W9-BFK-784

SNAKES
and other
REPTILES
of the
SOUTHWEST

by Erik D. Stoops & Annette Wright

GOLDEN WEST
PUBLISHERS

Cover design—The Book Studio

Front Cover Photo—Mohave Rattlesnake, by Hank Saunders/Stock Stock

Back Cover Photos—Durango Mountain Kingsnake by Joe Pierce, all others by Jeffrey
Howland.

Library of Congress Cataloging-in-Publication Data
Stoops, Erik D.,
 Snakes and Other Reptiles of the Southwest / by Erik Stoops and Annette Wright.
  p.   cm.
 Includes bibliographical references and index.
 ISBN 0-914846-79-5
  1. Reptiles—Southwestern States. 2. Snakes—Southwestern States.
I. Wright, Annette,   II. Title.
QL653.S68S75 1992   92-35815
597.9'0979—dc20   CIP

Printed in the United States of America

3rd Edition ©1996

Copyright ©1993 by Erik D. Stoops and Annette Wright. All rights reserved. This book
or any portion thereof, may not be reproduced in any form, except for review purposes,
without the written permission of the publisher.

Information in this book is deemed to be authentic and accurate by authors and publisher.
However, they disclaim any liability incurred in connection with the use of information
appearing in this book.

Golden West Publishers, Inc.
4113 N. Longview Ave.
Phoenix, AZ 85014, USA
(602) 265-4392

*Golden West Publishers books are available at special discounts to schools, clubs,
organizations and businesses for use as fund-raisers, premiums and special promotions.
Send inquiry to Director of Marketing.*

DEDICATION

This book is dedicated to the Boy Scouts and Girl Scouts of America—we are truly inspired by your love for the land and your fascination and respect for all of its living creatures.

"The Desert: mystical and magical, lonely and arid, but always full of color and living creatures."

Erik D. Stoops

ACKNOWLEDGEMENTS

We would like to thank: Donald and Shay Hamper, Joe Pierce, Tom Wright, Kirt Messick, Sherrie Stoops, Alesha Stoops, Corrine Konz, Helen Carlos, Al and Lorraine Lajoie, Melissa and Heather Benvenuti, Darryl Palmer, James Richmond, Kim Frazer, Norm Kayne, Gail and Dominick Barbera, Ryan Field and all the others who gave us their support.

Our special thanks to: The Arizona Game and Fish Department, Mickey Olson of the Wildlife World Zoo, Marge Wright of the Arizona Humane Society, Dale Belcher of the Rio Grande Zoological Park, The Prescott Zoo, Howard Lawler of the Arizona-Sonora Desert Museum, The Phoenix Zoo, The Arizona Herpetological Association, The Arizona Poison Control Center, Phoenix Children's Hospital, Good Samaritan Regional Medical Center, Cecil Schwalbe of the University of Arizona, Arizona State University, Phoenix Public Libraries, and Delia Perez, a very special friend.

And a very special thank you: to the students, teachers, parents, and other educators of the southwest that have allowed us to share with them our fascination with the world of reptiles.

We would like to acknowledge: Jeffrey Howland, Herpetologist, for his assistance in reviewing and updating information for this second printing.

CONTENTS

INTRODUCTION

The southwestern United States is comprised of lands of much diversity. From the coastal beaches of California, and sun-dried deserts of Arizona, to the rocky hills of New Mexico and evergreen forests of Texas, we can find a variety of habitats that are home to an equally diverse population of wildlife. Possibly the most unique members of our wildlife community in the Southwest are the REPTILES. Reptiles: snakes, lizards, turtles, tortoises, and crocodilians, are distinct in many ways among other animals and within their own members as well. First, reptiles are **cold-blooded**; that is, their body warmth is obtained from contact with the air and surrounding environment. Mammals, on the other hand, have a constant internal temperature controlled by their own bodily functions. Secondly, the outer skin surface of reptiles is comprised of **scales** or a leather-like hide rather than of fur or feathers.

This book is divided into three sections: SNAKES, TORTOISES and LIZARDS. Each section begins by describing characteristics of each family, then is broken down into information related to the different species found in that family. Although crocodilians are indeed reptiles, they are not found in the Southwest, so are not discussed. Keep in mind that there are literally thousands of different reptiles known. We have combined many of these reptiles to avoid redundant information. Also, the classifications and scientific naming of many of the reptiles are frequently changed by taxonomists in light of new information or the discovery of new color-variations or subspecies, and this book may not reflect all of the changes that have recently been made.

(Scientific names confirmed through reference: *Standard Common and Current Scientific Names for North American Amphibians and Reptiles*, 3rd Edition, Joseph T. Collins, editor and herpetologist, University of Kansas.)

IDENTIFICATION

When identifying reptiles, or for that matter, any animals at all, you must consider any and all physical characteristics as well as the general location at which the animal is found (its range of occurrence). Using turtles as an example, the physical characteristics that are used to identify them include:

Their general color and any pattern they might have on the carapace, plastron, head and limbs.

The size and shape of the carapace—is it highly domed, or is it flat? How are the shields arranged?

What does the plastron, or bottom shell, look like, and does it have special features such as notches or specially shaped plates. What color is it?

How long is the neck, and how does it retract into the shell?

Is the nose flattened or pointed? What do the tail and limbs look like?

All these questions are considered when turtles are identified. After one is identified, it must then be placed into a category as follows:

The ORDER that all turtles are placed under is Testudine, or Chelonia, depending on which scientist you speak to, which is further broken down into FAMILIES of turtles having similar characteristics, such as FAMILY Testudinidae; the tortoises..

Each kind of turtle is then named with a COMMON NAME, such as Box Turtle, and with a scientific name comprised of a GENUS and a SPECIES; for example, Genus-*Terrapene,* Species-*terrapene ornata.*

Different color variations or other differences may cause an individual to be further placed into a classification known as a SUBSPECIES. This scientific naming system is the same all over the world. Therefore, even if the common name changes from country to country, the scientific name will be the same.

The above scientific naming system also applies to the identification process of the lizards and snakes. Knowing this system will assist you in the identification of the reptiles of the Southwest.

We now invite you to explore with us

the world of the

Snakes and other Reptiles

of the Southwest

SNAKES

When we look at the evolution of snakes and of reptiles in general, we see that snakes are actually recent arrivals to the reptile class, which has been around for millions of years. It has been proven that snakes are descended from the lizards and still have many similarities to them.

There are both "primitive" and "modern" snakes. The primitive snakes have features that are quite similar to the lizards from which they are descended. For example, the Boids, a family of snakes that is considered the most primitive, have the remnants of legs and pelvic bones that appear as bony "spurs" located near their tails.

What is a snake, anyway? We already know they are cold-blooded reptiles with a driving need to obtain warmth from the sun and earth in order to function. They eat, they breed, and they sun themselves. That's it, right? Well, there is much, much more that makes up a snake than most people ever consider.

First, snakes are totally without legs and have developed special means of locomotion. The Legless Lizards are also without legs, but are in no way as graceful and flexible as a snake. The scales along the bottom of a snake's body are flat and the underlying muscles are attached to ribs that are each connected to a single vertebra making up the backbone.

When a snake moves, the small vertebrae, the ribs, and the muscles move gracefully together to cause the bottom scales to curve slightly to obtain leverage on the ground and propel the snake in the direction it wishes to go. This whole action is highly complex and results in a snake being able to move swiftly in any direction.

The process in which all snakes consume their food is highly unique. Snakes do not chew and are unable to break the food into smaller pieces. They must swallow everything in one piece. The bones of the head and jaw are very loosely joined by muscles. The upper and lower jaws can be widely separated because they are not hinged to each other. The bottom jaw can be stretched apart sideways

Snakes are able to move gracefully on most surfaces, as demonstrated by this Sonoran Mountain Kingsnake. *(Photograph by Tom Wright)*

as well. The effect is that the jaw and head can be nearly separated to accommodate food items that are larger in diameter than the snake's own head. The teeth inside the mouth are curved and hook-like, and they help to pull the food into the throat.

There is one thing that snakes are truly not capable of, and that is hearing. Snakes do not have an ear structure that allows them to detect sounds. However, snakes have developed specializations that make up for this lack.

Snakes' tongues are their most important sensory organ—they use it to smell. When they flick out their tongues, they take small molecules of matter from the air into their mouth and analyze the matter using the "Jacobson's organ," which is their organ of smell. Most lizards also have this capability.

Snakes pick up even the mildest vibrations on the ground, which makes great sense, since they lie directly on it. Many snakes have pits or openings, on the front or sides of their heads that enable them to detect heat. Although snakes can see quite well if an object is close to them and moving, and are able to see colors as well, their eyesight is less important to them compared to the other senses. All in all, snakes are very well equipped to hunt down the small animals they consume.

Which brings us to how snakes are important to us. Snakes play a definite role in keeping a balance in the natural world by consuming the rodents and insects that are main causes of diseases such as "The Plague." Some species of snakes regularly consume other snakes, including venomous ones, which further maintains a balance in nature.

In the Southwest, there are many different kinds of snakes, some small and some large, some harmless and some exceptionally dangerous. All are useful to us in some way, and should be left undisturbed in their natural environment.

If a large or venomous snake is encountered in a human settlement, every attempt should be made to **move it** to a safe place within a radius of 1 mile. But if human lives are at stake, killing it may be one option. Killing any snake, venomous or not, in its natural environment will not only disrupt nature's balance, but is usually unnecessary.

Snakes will, without dispute, defend themselves if unable to escape or are cornered. But if given an opportunity, they will usually crawl away, often after a loud warning hiss or rattle. The key for us to avoiding injury is to give a snake every opportunity to escape and to not be a threat to them. While hiking, be alert for a snake's warning—tight coiling, hissing, or rattling and vibrating of the tail. Avoid threatening them—stand still! If you are interested in getting to know the snake, take a picture, but don't pick it up! Watch where you put your feet and hands, and don't step onto a patch of ground you can't survey with your eyes first. Believe me, if you step on, or even come close to stepping on a snake, you will get bit, since that is his only method of protecting himself at that point.

Please refer to the section on Rattlesnakes for methods of first aid treatment if a bite does occur.

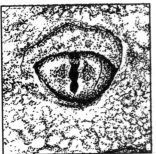 *Lizard with eyelids.*

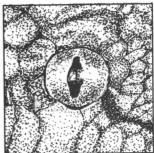

Snake without eyelids.

One primary difference between snakes and lizards is that snakes, without exception, do not have eyelids.   *(Illustration by Kirt M. Messick)*

BLIND SNAKES

Family Leptotyphlopidae

This family of snakes consists of one of the so-called primitive snakes and is truly a very basic type of snake. They are also called worm snakes because that is exactly how they appear—small, slender, and resembling worms. Their bodies are cylindrical, with the head and tail rounded and hard to identify as separate from the body.

The scales on the body are tiny and smooth. They don't have the enlarged scales on the bottom side of the body as do other snakes. They are not as flexible, and cannot stretch their jaw to the same degree as other snakes, which restricts them to eating only small insects such as termites and ants.

These snakes are probably the closest relatives of the lizards. If you were to x-ray one, you'd find evidence of bony structures that once were legs, and that the bones of the head resemble a lizard's.

These snakes are very tiny, seldom growing to more than 15 inches in length, which further makes them resemble worms. They have exceptionally small eyes that are often covered by a scale; they appear to have no eyes at all.

All species in this family are secretive burrowers that are seldom seen unless you happen to spot them as they emerge from their burrows at night. They are fully nocturnal. They are relatively common, and most household owners probably have several living underground near the base of their homes helping to control termites and ants.

COMMON NAME: **Western Blind Snake**

SCIENTIFIC NAME: *Leptotyphlops humilis*

IDENTIFICATION: Cylindrical in shape with smooth, glossy scales. May be brown, silver, purple, or pink without pattern. Has a small spine on the tip of its blunt tail.

HABITS: Lives underground, forages beneath the soil, rocks, and vegetation for ants and termites. Emerges on occasion to move to a different area and to search for a mate.

REPRODUCTION: Several females may lay their long, slender eggs in one nest, and most females will tend to the eggs until they hatch. Babies are approximately 3 inches in length. Adult length is 8 to 16 inches.

RANGE: Throughout the entire southwestern range.

RELATED SPECIES:

Texas Blind Snake *(Leptotyphlops dulcis)*
Range is wider over the Texas area.

Western Blind Snakes are very infrequently seen above ground, but occasionally emerge on warm nights.. *(Photograph by Jeffrey Howland)*

BOAS AND PYTHONS

Family Boidae

The Boas and Pythons are probably the most well-known family of snakes. The majority of people have probably heard of the infamous Boa Constrictors of South America, and of the Giant Pythons of Africa and Asia. But there is a vast number of species in this family, many of which are quite small.

Most Boas and Pythons are found in tropical areas in South America and Asia. The United States is home to two kinds of Boas, which are smaller than their giant relatives of the tropics, but have all the same characteristics.

Boids, as members of this family are commonly called, have muscular bodies and short tails. They use these strong muscles to constrict the prey they catch—suffocating it before consuming it. They have the large scales on the underside typical of all land-dwelling snakes. These enable them to move fairly rapidly and efficiently despite their bulk.

One common means of identifying the Boids, as separate from another family of snakes, is that they possess spurs, which are bony structures located on either side of the anal opening at the base of the tail. These spurs are the remnants of hind leg and hip bones that snakes' ancestors possessed millions of years ago. Males often have larger spurs, and may even use them in the mating process. Boas give live birth, and Pythons lay eggs.

COMMON NAME: **Rosy Boa**

SCIENTIFIC NAME: *Lichanura trivirgata*

IDENTIFICATION: A stout Boa with smooth, glossy scales. Color is tan, gray, pink, yellow, or even red with 3 brown stripes and dark blotches or speckles. May be more brilliantly striped in rose or yellow, depending on subspecies. They grow to an adult length of 2 to 3 feet.

HABITS: This snake is shy and rather secretive, hunting at night for rodents and small birds. Will seldom bite, preferring to coil in a tight ball with its head tucked into the body coils as a means of protection. Although brightly colored, the pattern of colors provides camouflage for the snake among the rocks and brush. They are not common, but may be found near streams and small springs in canyons, rocky foothills, and gorges.

REPRODUCTION: Males use their long, curved spurs to stroke the female during mating. Females give live birth to 2 to 6 young in the fall. The babies are approximately 10 inches at birth.

RANGE: Southern Arizona and California.

Rosy Boas have the stout body of most Boas, and use constriction to capture and subdue their prey.   *(Photograph by Jeffrey Howland)*

TYPICAL SNAKES

Family Colubridae

At least two-thirds of all snakes fall into this family, including the majority of all snakes found in the Southwest. This family, commonly called the colubrids, can be broken down into two categories: Those that are non-poisonous versus the poisonous colubrids.

Since this group of snakes is so large, and the snakes in it have such a variety of features and habits, it is hard to discuss the similarities that cause them to be all placed in this family. Biologists have found it challenging to organize the many diverse species into orderly groups.

Since there is such a variety of features and colors in the snakes of this family, most of the species we know have been further broken down into subspecies—the snakes having minor color, scale pattern, or range variations only. In order to avoid redundant information, we will not describe all subspecies in full, and related species will be grouped together.

Colubrids are the "typical" snakes, and are also considered harmless and beneficial.
(Illustration by James Richmond)

COMMON NAME: **Western Garter Snake (Aquatic)**

SCIENTIFIC NAME: *Thamnophis couchii*

IDENTIFICATION: A slender, supple snake with highly variable markings, usually some combination of gray and olive with occasional stripes, spots, or blotches. Grows to an adult length of 2 to 4 feet.

HABITS: This particular species is fully aquatic and is active during the day. Feeds on fish, amphibians, worms, and larvae. Found in any permanent body of water from sea level to mountainous regions.

REPRODUCTION: Females give live birth to up to 25 young.

RANGE: Throughout California and western Nevada.

RELATED SPECIES: There are several other types of garter snakes also within our range:

> Western Terrestrial Garter Snake *(Thamnophis elegans)*
> Range: Includes northern areas of California, Nevada, New Mexico, and
> Arizona.
> Features: Basks on land, and takes to water only to protect itself. Eats
> most animal matter.

> Black-Necked Garter Snake *(Thamnophis cyrtopsis)*
> Range: Utah, Colorado, New Mexico, Texas, and Arizona.

Western Terrestrial Garter Snakes, are slender, active, and alert snakes found over a wide area. *(Photograph by Jeffrey Howland)*

Features: Large black blotches and stripe on neck. Does not swim below the water, but swims on the surface instead. Primarily a land-dweller.

Checkered Garter Snake *(Thamnophis marcianus)*
Range: Southern California and Arizona, east through New Mexico and Texas.
Features: Black checkered pattern. Resides near, but not necessarily in, water.

Mexican Garter Snake *(Thamnophis eques)*
Range: Arizona and New Mexico.
Features: Body has more bulk than other Garter Snakes. Aquatic. Preys on frogs.

Western Ribbon Snake *(Thamnophis proximus)*
Range: Some subspecies found in the Texas and New Mexico areas of our range.
Features: Very slender and streamlined. Dwells on land areas on the shores of small bodies of water.

This particular Black-Necked Garter Snake has a black neck, but also has a pattern of distinct stripes. *(Photograph by Jeffrey Howland)*

Narrow-Headed Garter Snake *(Thamnophis rufipunctatus)*
Range: Arizona and New Mexico.
Features: Does not look like most Garter Snakes; has a very narrow, streamlined head. Can be found lying on the bottom floor of clear, rocky streams, and is primarily a forest dweller. Eats fish.

Common Garter Snake (Thamnophis sirtalis)
Range: Some subspecies found in California, Nevada, and separately in Texas, and New Mexico areas.
Features: Most commonly encountered snake. Inhabits most areas associated with bodies of water. Has many subspecies.

COMMON NAME: **Racer**

SCIENTIFIC NAME: *Coluber constrictor*

IDENTIFICATION: Racers are large, slender snakes that are commonly found in the eastern as well as western United States. There are many color variations. The western types are generally black, brown, or grayish-green. Adults are without pattern, and only neonates have a blotched pattern that fades with age.

HABITS: These snakes are fast and agile, as their name suggests. They are frequently encountered swiftly crossing roads with their head held up as they survey the territory. Because they are so active, they are always hungry, and hunt for rodents and lizards during the day. If frightened, they will quiver their tail tip and mimic the rattling behavior of the Rattlesnakes. If captured, will thrash and twist to escape and will bite as well.

REPRODUCTION: Females lay from 6 to 20 eggs in midsummer.

RANGE: Most areas of continental United States. Two in our range.

COMMON NAME: **Coachwhip**

SCIENTIFIC NAME: *Masticophis flagellum*

IDENTIFICATION: These snakes are large, growing to a length of 4 to 8 feet. Those that are found in our range are usually tan, brown, yellow, or gray, with occasional specimens being all black. Some are patternless, and some have crossbands or streaks on the body and neck.

HABITS: The Coachwhip not only resembles a rope or whip, but is one of the fastest moving snakes in the world. Because they are so active, they must frequently hunt for the rodents, snakes, lizards, and insects they consume. They have been accused of whipping their prey to death, which they do not. They are very efficient hunters. May be found in desert, grassland, and most open areas.

REPRODUCTION: Female lays 4 to 15 rough-textured eggs.

Coachwhip snakes resemble a rope or whip and are one of the fastest moving snakes in the world.

(Photograph by Terry Odegaard)

RELATED SPECIES: The Coachwhip is only one of several snakes called Whipsnakes. They are slender, agile snakes frequently seen in our range.

Striped Whipsnake *(Masticophis taeniatus)*
Range: Texas, Nevada, Arizona, Utah and New Mexico.
Features: Has stripes. Subspecies have other color variations as well.

Striped Racer *(Masticophis lateralis)*
Range: California.
Features: Brown or black with a yellow or orange stripe on either side
of the body.

Sonoran Whipsnake *(Masticophis bilineatus)*
Range: Arizona and New Mexico.

Ground Snakes come in a variety of color patterns; this one is banded. They are very small and adept at hiding. *(Photograph by Jeffrey Howland)*

COMMON NAME: **Ground Snake**

SCIENTIFIC NAME: *Sonora semiannulata*

IDENTIFICATION: Small in size with glossy scales. May be gray, brown, or reddish in color, without pattern or with blotches, bars, stripes, or a combination of some sort. Adults grow to a length of only 8 to 18 inches.

HABITS: This small, secretive snake is often called a Red Racer, and many people confuse them with baby Racers, which they actually resemble only slightly. These snakes are burrowers and are found in sandy wooded or prairie areas along river beds and even in backyards. They eat insects, spiders, scorpions, and centipedes, so they are useful to have around.

REPRODUCTION: Females lay 1 to 6 eggs. Babies are 4 to 5 inches long when born.

RANGE: Includes Nevada, California, Arizona, New Mexico, and Texas.

COMMON NAME: **Glossy Snake**

SCIENTIFIC NAME: *Arizona elegans*

IDENTIFICATION: These snakes have smooth, glossy scales, but otherwise resemble Gopher Snakes, with a general color of brown, tan, and even pinkish hues intermixed with black or gray blotches. However, the pattern has a somewhat muted or bleached appearance, which is why this snake is sometimes called the Faded snake. Adults grow to a length of 3 to 5 feet.

HABITS: This snake is primarily a burrower, but may be seen crossing roads or other open areas in the early evening. They hunt for lizards and occasionally small mammals. Found in sandy desert as well as woodland areas.

REPRODUCTION: Females lay up to 20 very elongated eggs.

RANGE: Texas, New Mexico, Arizona, and California.

Glossy Snakes, as their name suggests, have smooth scales, and the pattern is somewhat faded or bleached. (*Photograph by Jeffrey Howland*)

COMMON NAME: **Banded Sand Snake**

SCIENTIFIC NAME: *Chilomeniscus cinctus*

IDENTIFICATION: Adults are tiny, growing to a length of only 10 inches. The scales are smooth and shiny, and the snake is generally yellow or orange with black or brown rings. The nose is somewhat flat and the head and neck are approximately the same width.

HABITS: The flat nose, or shovelnose, is used for burrowing in the fine sand in the desert as well as hillside areas. They have valves in their nose that prevent sand from entering when they move through fine sand. They consume centipedes, cockroaches, and other insects that have soft bodies. They are not commonly encountered and may be easily confused with the venomous Coral snake, which is also small and banded.

REPRODUCTION: Females lay eggs which are very small. Baby snakes are 3 to 4 inches long at birth, very large compared to the size of the adults.
RANGE: Arizona and Southern California.

COMMON NAME: **Ringneck Snake**

SCIENTIFIC NAME: *Diadophis punctatus*

IDENTIFICATION: Adults are small, growing only to a length of 12 to 28 inches. They are slender with a bright color pattern of gray, black, brown, or olive above and red, yellow, or orange below. May have a ring of orange, yellow, or cream around its neck. Scales are smooth.

HABITS: These are secretive snakes that hide under fallen logs or rocks in moist areas of forests, brushlands, and hillsides and occasionally near streams. When frightened, will raise their tails and show their colorful undersides in an attempt to ward off their enemies. If captured, will release a strong-smelling musk or defecate. They eat worms, lizards, newborn snakes, and salamanders.

REPRODUCTION: Females lay elongated eggs in sites shared by other female Ringneck Snakes.

RANGE: Most found in our range are in California. The Regal Ringneck Snake is found in Utah, Nevada, and Arizona, New Mexico, and Texas.

COMMON NAME: **Western Hognose Snake**

SCIENTIFIC NAME: *Heterodon nasicus*

IDENTIFICATION: This snake has a very unusual appearance with a stout body and a wide neck. The snout is upturned and pointed. They are tan, gray, or brown with light blotches, and they have dark blotches on their undersides as well.

HABITS: They burrow in loose soil in the prairie areas where they are found. They are unlike other burrowing snakes, which are usually slender. They also have a unique means of defense—they will expand their neck, much like a Cobra's hood, and hiss loudly. If that doesn't work, they will turn over and "play dead," and if you right them, they will just turn over again. They are efficient hunters of buried toads, reptile eggs, and lizards and will eat birds and rodents.

REPRODUCTION: Females lay from 5 to 20 elongated eggs.

RANGE: Texas, New Mexico, Arizona.

The Western Hognose Snake has a pointed upturned snout.
(Photograph by Terry Odegaard)

COMMON NAME: **Western Hooknose Snake**

SCIENTIFIC NAME: *Gyalopion canum*

IDENTIFICATION: Identified by its pointed, upturned snout. Usually light brown with darker brown crossbands and 2 obvious crossbands on the head. Grows to a length of 10 to 14 inches, making it one of the smallest snakes in our range.

HABITS: Found in desert areas that have heavy areas of brush or trees, as well as in mountain woodland areas. Probably a burrower, they come to the surface at night after a period of rain. They hunt for insects, spiders, and scorpions. Has only rarely been encountered.

REPRODUCTION: Habits unknown. Females lay eggs.

RANGE: Southern Arizona, New Mexico, and Texas.

RELATED SPECIES:

> Desert Hooknose Snake *(Gyalopion quadrangulare)*
> Range: Extreme southern Arizona.
> Features: Color reddish-brown with a large blotch on the head. Very
> rare, secretive, and nocturnal. Burrows. Primarily a desert
> dweller, but also found in dry, forested areas.

COMMON NAME: **Longnose Snake**

SCIENTIFIC NAME: *Rhinocheilus lecontei*

IDENTIFICATION: Tri-colored with red, yellow, or cream, and saddle-shaped black blotches. Black and white specimens have also been seen. Scales are smooth. The nose is pointed and may be slightly upturned. Adults grow to a length of 2 to 3 feet.

HABITS: These snakes burrow in loose soil and are primarily active at night, when they hunt for lizards, small snakes, reptile eggs, and rodents. When captured, will first hide the head and tightly coil its body, and vibrate the tail to mimic rattling. If this is not successful in getting rid of the enemy, it will release secretions from its anal opening, which may be bloody with a strong odor.

REPRODUCTION: Females lay 4 to 8 eggs in burrows.

RANGE: New Mexico, Texas, Arizona, Utah, Nevada, and California..

Longnose Snakes have an attractive tri-colored pattern that provides some degree of camouflage. *(Photograph by Jeffrey Howland)*

COMMON NAME: **Western Shovelnose Snake**

SCIENTIFIC NAME: *Chionactis occipitalis*

IDENTIFICATION: Generally light yellow with many dark crossbands and possibly orange or reddish crossbands as well. The snout is flattened, and the nose juts past the lower jaw. The scales are smooth.

HABITS: These snakes have small valves that close off the nostrils, and a flat belly that enables them to burrow and move quickly through the sand. They eat insects, scorpions, and centipedes. They are active at night and can be encountered crossing roads in the sandy desert or brush areas, as well as in dry riverbeds and rocky areas.

REPRODUCTION: Lays up to 4 eggs in midsummer.

RANGE: Nevada, California, Arizona.

RELATED SPECIES:

> Sonoran Shovelnose Snake *(Chionactis palarostris)*
> Range: Organ-Pipe National Monument, Arizona. RARE
> Features: Yellow with and red and black crossbands.

Shovelnose Snakes are named for their flattened snout and specialized head that allows them to burrow quickly through sand. *(Photograph by Donald Hamper)*

COMMON NAME: **Western Patchnose Snake**

SCIENTIFIC NAME: *Salvadora hexalepis*

IDENTIFICATION: Color generally gray with lighter colored broad stripes. There is a large triangular scale that is curved over the end of the snout. Scales are smooth. Adults grow to a length of 2 to 3 feet.

HABITS: These snakes are agile and active during the day. They are able to tolerate high temperatures. While most snakes would be in shelter to get out of the heat, these snakes will be hunting lizards, young snakes, and small mice.

REPRODUCTION: Lays up to 10 eggs in midsummer.

RANGE: California, Nevada, Arizona, and Utah.

This Big Bend Patchnose Snake is much like the Western Patchnose Snake in that it can live in high temperature climates.   *(Photograph by Jeffrey Howland)*

RELATED SPECIES:
> Big Bend Patchnose Snake *(Salvadora deserticola)*
> Range: Southern Texas, New Mexico, and Arizona.
>
> Mountain Patchnose Snake *(Salvadora grahamiae)*
> Range: Mountain areas of Southern Arizona, New Mexico, Texas.

This Mountain Patchnose Snake prefers areas of higher elevations with cooler climates and rock outcroppings. (*Photograph by Jeffrey Howland*)

COMMON NAME: **Saddled Leafnose Snake**

SCIENTIFIC NAME: *Phyllorhynchus browni*

IDENTIFICATION: Color generally light pink with large, dark, saddle-shaped blotches. A triangular scale curves over the tip of the nose. Pupils of the eyes are vertical.

HABITS: These are secretive, nocturnal snakes that are not common, but have been seen crossing roads after dark in the summer rainy months. They reside in brushy and rocky desert areas, and eat lizards. When frightened, will coil and hiss as well as strike in a pose much like a Rattlesnake.

REPRODUCTION: Lays up to 5 large, elongated eggs in summer.

RANGE: Southern Arizona.

RELATED SPECIES:
Spotted Leafnose Snake *(Phyllorhynchus decurtatus)*
Range: Nevada, California, Arizona.
Features: Has many, rounded blotches that resemble spots. They eat
Geckos (lizards).

Gopher Snakes are large, active, and consume a large amount of rodents.
(Photograph by Jeffrey Howland)

COMMON NAME: Gopher Snake

SCIENTIFIC NAME: *Pituophis catenifer* or *Pituophis melanoleucus*

IDENTIFICATION: One of the largest snakes in our range; adults grow to a length of up to 8 feet. Body is muscular and the snout is somewhat pointed with an enlarged scale on the front of the nose. Background color is usually light with brown, black, or reddish blotches. The Santa Cruz subspecies is dwarf—grows to only 2 to 3 feet.

HABITS: Active during the day in cool weather and at night during the hot summer months. Will hide from predators under rocks and in animal burrows. They are extremely desirable to have around, since they consume large amounts of rodents. When frightened, they hiss loudly and strike at the intruder. May vibrate tail like a Rattlesnake.

REPRODUCTION: Females lay 5 to 20 elongated eggs under rocks or in burrows.

RANGE: Open desert and woodlands throughout our range.

This San Diego Gopher Snake has an unusual pattern which likely helps to camouflage the snake in its environment. *(Photograph by Jeffrey Howland)*

COMMON NAME: **Trans-Pecos Rat Snake**

SCIENTIFIC NAME: *Bogertophis subocularis*

IDENTIFICATION: Yellow, orange, or tan in color with numerous H-shaped blotches of dark brown. The H's may connect along the sides of the snake to form stripes. This Rat Snake is unusual in that the eyes are large and protruding. Adults may reach a length of 4 to 5 feet.

HABITS: Like other Rat Snakes, it is active during the day in winter and early spring and in the evening hours when the weather is warm. Hides in burrows or rock crevices to escape from the summer heat. They are constrictors, and feed on rodents, lizards, and birds.

REPRODUCTION: Females lay up to 7 elongated, leathery eggs.

RANGE: Texas and southern New Mexico.

RELATED SPECIES:

    Green Rat Snake *(Senticolis triaspis)*
    Range: Southeastern Arizona. Rarely encountered.
    Features: Another, unusual Rat Snake in our range that is green or olive without pattern. Has a long, square head. Resides near streams in rocky hillsides and mountainous areas. Climbs trees. Adults may grow to a length of 3 to 4 feet.

The Trans-Pecos Rat Snake has a unique pattern of H-Shaped blotches and bulging eyes.
(Photograph by Jeffrey Howland)

COMMON NAME: **Common Kingsnake**

SCIENTIFIC NAME: *Lampropeltis getula*

IDENTIFICATION: This is the black and white Kingsnake commonly seen in our range. Pattern is extremely variable with crossbands, stripes, blotches, speckles or a combination on a background of dark brown or black. The scales are smooth, and the head is small and rounded.

HABITS: They are commonly found in desert, prairie, mountain, woodland, or even marshy areas. They are active during the day most of the year. In summer they are active at night. Kingsnakes constrict their prey, and they consume lizards, rodents, birds, and other snakes. They have the ability to kill and consume poisonous snakes, since they are immune to the venom.

REPRODUCTION: Females lay up to 20 elongated eggs in either spring or summer, depending on their location.

RANGE: Includes all states in our range, depending on the subspecies.

RELATED SPECIES: There are several other kinds of Kingsnakes that are within our range as well:

Sonoran Mountain Kingsnake *(Lampropeltis pyromelana)*
Range: Utah, Nevada, and Arizona.

The Desert Kingsnake like all Kingsnakes, is immune to the venom of rattlesnakes. (Photograph by Jeffrey Howland)

Features: Tri-colored Kingsnake with bands of red, black, white, or yellow. The snout is always light in color. The red and light bands always touch the black bands, which is how they are identified as different from the Coral Snake. Found in mountain areas, especially forests and canyons.

California Mountain Kingsnake *(Lampropeltis zonata)*

Range: California, Nevada.

Features: Also tri-colored, but with red, white, and black only. Snout is black. Red bands next to black bands. Found in pine or redwood forests.

The California Mountain Kingsnake has red, black, and white bands. (Photograph by Erik Stoops)

Baja Mountain Kingsnakes are often mistaken for Coral Snakes and killed, as are other tri-colored snakes. *(Photograph by Joe Pierce)*

COMMON NAME: **Gray-Banded Kingsnake**

SCIENTIFIC NAME: *Lampropeltis alterna*

IDENTIFICATION: A slender Kingsnake that averages 3 feet in length when adult. Although most individuals have the typical banded pattern of gray alternating with red bands or blotches, many color variations have been noted, including patterns without any gray color at all.

HABITS: These Kingsnakes are highly secretive and come out at night to hunt for the lizards, frogs, small snakes and the small rodents they consume. They are much more common than once was believed and can be encountered in flat desert areas, crossing roads after the summer rains, in rocky canyons, and in forest areas in the mountains.

REPRODUCTION: Females lay an average of 5 eggs beneath stones or logs in moist locations. Neonates may have little resemblance to their parents or siblings.

RANGE: Trans-Pecos region of Texas into Mexico.

Milk Snakes are related to Kingsnakes, and often have a repetitious pattern of color bands that are used to identify them. *(Photograph by Jeffrey Howland)*

COMMON NAME: **Milk Snake**

SCIENTIFIC NAME: *Lampropeltis triangulum*

IDENTIFICATION: There are two color variations. Those in our range are ringed with red or orange, black, and yellow or white. The other variation is found in those to the east. The pattern is predictable—there is a light colored band at the neck, then a black-bordered red band, then a light ring, and so on. Adults average 2 to 3 feet.

HABITS: They are much like Kingsnakes and are able to consume venomous snakes. They are more secretive than Kingsnakes and are out more at night. Found under logs and fallen branches in a wide variety of settings, including plains, forests, deserts, or waterways.

REPRODUCTION: Females lay up to 15 eggs.

RANGE: Includes Texas, with small, rare populations in Utah, Colorado, and Arizona.

VENOMOUS COLUBRIDS

There is a small group of snakes in our range that are indeed part of the general family of Colubrids previously described, but have enlarged, grooved teeth (fangs) and a mild venom to subdue their prey. For this reason, they deserve special mention.

Venom is a chemical compound that many animals use in the capture and digestion of prey. Venom, depending on the potency, causes paralysis and/or death in a short period of time and will begin the process of digestion before the prey is swallowed. In snakes, venom is injected into the prey by fangs, which are hollow. However, just as there are different types and potency of venom, there are also different kinds of fangs. Some are large and located in the front of the upper jaw (the Vipers), and some are located far in the back of the jaw, being either very small or large depending on the species.

The snakes we are to discuss here are the Rear-fanged snakes in our range, whose venom is designed to subdue small prey and is actually a strong form of saliva, rather than the potent venom we know of in the other poisonous snakes. The venom is mild, and the fangs are in the rear and can only be utilized if the snake bites, holds on, and tries to swallow what it has in its mouth. Thus, these snakes are considered essentially as harmless to man as are the non-venomous species we know, but only if left strictly alone.

COMMON NAME: **Night Snake**

SCIENTIFIC NAME: *Hypsiglena torquata*

IDENTIFICATION: Adults are 1 to 2 feet in length. This is a slender snake with a cylindrical body. Color is tan, yellow, or gray with dark blotches. There is a large blotch on either side of the neck.

HABITS: This is a rarely-encountered, highly secretive snake that is fully nocturnal. It hides under rocks or leaf litter in sandy or rocky areas of the desert, brush, or woodland areas. Has large, grooved teeth in the back of the upper jaw to hold lizards and frogs in the mouth while the toxic saliva begins the process of digestion and subdues the animal.

REPRODUCTION: Females lay up to 6 eggs in early summer.

Night Snakes are seldom seen because they are nocturnal; hunting during late evening and night. They are very secretive. *(Photograph by Jeffrey Howland)*

COMMON NAME: **Western Black-Headed Snake**

SCIENTIFIC NAME: *Tantilla planiceps*

IDENTIFICATION: One of several kinds of Black-headed Snakes in our range. Has an olive, gray, tan, or brown body with a slight orange color near the tail. The head and neck are black.

HABITS: It is found near streams, woodlands, and grassy areas of the desert as well as the lower hilly or mountain areas. They are burrowers, and come onto the surface at night especially after the summer rains. They eat small lizards and insects, as well as centipedes. They are rear-fanged and have mildly venomous saliva.

REPRODUCTION: Lays up to 3 eggs in early summer.

RANGE: Colorado, Nevada, Utah, and California.

RELATED SPECIES:

Plains Black-Headed Snake *(Tantilla nigriceps)*
Range: Includes Colorado, Texas, New Mexico, Arizona.
Features: Only top surface of head is black. Burrows deeply during
hibernation.
Mexican Black-Headed Snake *(Tantilla atriceps)*
Range: Arizona, New Mexico, and Texas.
Features: Belly orange. Top of head is black.

COMMON NAME: **Mexican Vine Snake**

SCIENTIFIC NAME: *Oxybelis aeneus*

IDENTIFICATION: Extremely slender, resembling a trailing vine. Has a narrow head, and the snout is pointed. The forward parts of the body are yellowish-brown or tan that darkens to a gray or brown color towards the tail. Adults grow to a length of 3 to 5 feet.

HABITS: These snakes are arboreal (tree dwelling). On occasion, they crawl on the ground with their head held high in search for lizards. Their rear fangs inject a mild venom into the prey that quickly immobilizes the animal. They are found in only a small area in our range, inhabiting hilly areas and canyons with trees and brush.

REPRODUCTION: Females lay only 3 to 5 very elongated eggs.

RANGE: Extreme southern Arizona into Mexico.

COMMON NAME: **Lyre Snake**

SCIENTIFIC NAME: *Trimorphodon biscutatus*

IDENTIFICATION: Light brown or gray with darker saddle-shaped blotches that are smaller on the sides. This snake is slim and is primarily identified by the presence of a lyre-shaped mark (violin shaped) on the head. The pupils are vertical, giving this snake a cat-eyed appearance.

HABITS: These snakes are active at night in search of small mammals, lizards, and birds which they subdue by means of rear fangs and a mild venom. Not a common snake, but may be seen in hilly, rocky areas and canyons as well as desert and forest areas.

REPRODUCTION: Females lay 4 to 12 eggs in summer.

RANGE: California, Arizona, New Mexico, and Texas and the southernmost parts of Utah and Nevada.

CORAL SNAKES

Family Elapidae

This family, commonly called the Elapids, is a large group of venomous snakes that are made up of the Cobras, Mambas, Kraits, Coral Snakes and many others. In our country, only the Coral Snakes are represented.

The primary qualification that places snakes in this category is the presence of hollow fangs in the front of the upper jaw that are not moveable. Unlike the fangs of the Vipers, these snakes have fangs that do not fold flat when the mouth is closed and are therefore small in size. The venom, however, is highly potent and affects the nervous system of the victim causing paralysis.

Again, the venom of Coral Snakes, and, in fact all other venomous snakes, is primarily for digestion. It immobilizes the prey and begins the process of digestion. When a snake bites in defense, venom may or may not be administered—if not, it is called a "dry" bite. As a matter of fact, although having a highly potent venom, the Coral Snake is so small it would have to **bite down and hold on** in order to inflict injury. The fangs can only be inserted into tissue in a **downward** direction and not in the typical viper striking position, which is forward with the mouth open. So unless you plan to stick your hands or feet in a Coral Snake's range, you should be safe. Unfortunately, children playing in the soil can be bitten by a Coral Snake, and may not even know they have been bitten until much later.

The reactions experienced by those bitten by a Coral Snake may be as follows:

1. Small fang marks will be present, but there will be little or no pain at the site of the wound.
2. Apprehension and weakness may occur several hours after the injury with nausea and vomiting, salivation, convulsions, and eventually paralysis. The victim will be awake and not disoriented.

First-aid treatment entails the following:

1. Transport victim to the hospital immediately. Do not wait for symptoms to appear.
2. If symptoms occur, but the bite has not been confirmed, check the hands and feet for fang marks.
3. Do not suck on the wound, since that will cause more venom to be absorbed. Wash the wound with plain water.

In the hospital:

1. Physicians will mechanically support breathing and heart rate if needed.
2. Skin testing will be done to make sure victim is not allergic, and antivenom may be given by intravenous injection.
3. Victim may remain hospitalized for at least 24 hours.

This particular Coral Snake is not an Arizona Coral Snake, but still shows the yellow bands next to the red bands. (see color plate)   *(Photograph by Donald Hamper)*

COMMON NAME: **Arizona Coral Snake**

SCIENTIFIC NAME: *Micruroides euryxanthus*

IDENTIFICATION: This is a slender, tri-colored snake with glossy scales and a blunt nose. A pattern of wide red and black bands separated by yellow or white rings circle the body. The head is black.

HABITS: A common lyric used to differentiate a Coral Snake from other tri-colored snakes is:

> If Red touches Yellow, it can kill a fellow
> If Red touches Black, it's okay for Jack

Coral snakes are not commonly found. They come out at night from their daytime burrows in search of the small snakes they consume. When frightened, they will tuck their heads into their coils and raise the tail, making a popping sound with their anal opening. Preventing an injury is easy—DO NOT HANDLE. Although relatively rare, they can be found in rocky, hilly areas and dry river bottoms in the desert and low mountains.

REPRODUCTION: Females lay 1 to 3 eggs in midsummer.

RANGE: Central Arizona and extreme southwestern New Mexico.

PIT VIPERS

Family Viperidae

Those snakes that are members of the family Viperidae, also called the Vipers, are characterized as such due to the presence of large, hollow fangs in the front of the upper jaw that are used to inject venom into their prey. These fangs are different from those of the Elapids, such as the Coral Snakes and Cobras, in

Most Pit Vipers have wide heads, however using that feature is not the most reliable way to identify these snakes. *(Photograph by Tom Wright)*

that they are attached to the jaw bone and are moveable. When a Viper strikes at its prey, the fangs become erect, and a stabbing motion rather than a biting down motion is used to inject the venom. When not in use, the fangs are housed in protective sheaths and fold flat into the roof of the mouth.

The family Viperidae is further broken down into subfamilies. The subfamily of Vipers found in the Southwest, are those snakes called the Pit Vipers or the Crotalines. These snakes are different from the other Vipers in that they have a thermoreceptive (heat-sensitive) pit located between the nostril and the eye on each side of the head. These pits are quite different in appearance and function than, for example, those on the Boids, which are shallow pits located in the front of the nose area. The pits of the Crotalines are deep, and extend into the oral cavity. When these snakes hunt, they first use their tongues in the fashion of all snakes.

The snake will then turn his head towards the animal, at which time the pits will pick up infrared rays (heat waves) that emit from the body of the warm-blooded animal.

The snake essentially can triangulate these signals into a clear determination of where the animal is and how far away. The pits are extremely sensitive and can detect temperature changes as low as 1.5 to 2 degrees Fahrenheit. The snake then strikes rapidly and surely, injecting the venom into the animal. This family of snakes is not only one of the most highly advanced in terms of specialized features, but is also highly dangerous as well.

The venom, as previously discussed, is a complex mixture of enzymes which act in a digestive function. Not only will the venom cause the death of the prey animal, but it will begin the breakdown process of digestion even before the food is fully ingested. It is this property that causes injury in the unfortunate humans who have been bitten by a defensive Pit Viper.

This Western Diamondback Rattlesnake is communicating a very obvious defensive warning to stay away.   *(Photograph by Jeffrey Howland)*

In defense, these snakes can be highly dangerous. As they strike to protect themselves, the fangs are usually erected when the mouth is opened to bite. Rattling, random striking, and a coiled position usually preceeds a defensive bite. Although dry bites are common, since snakes can control the amount of venom injected, all bites should be treated with the assumption that envenomation has occurred. We point out again, that snakes will bite in **defense** if they feel threatened. The key to avoiding injury is to prevent it in the first place by avoiding situations where a snake will be made to feel threatened. Snakes do not hunt down people in order to bite them, but do indeed bite if they have no other recourse and no way to escape.

PREVENTION OF SNAKEBITE INJURIES

1. Watch where you walk or sit. Don't step over rocks or logs; step on top of them first in order to get a clear view of what is on the other side before moving on.

2. Wear high-topped shoes or boots with loose-fitting long pants with the cuff over the tops of the shoes. If a snake does bite, it may get caught on the material without inflicting a skin wound.

3. If you hear a snake hiss or rattle, stand still, and allow it the choice and opportunity to move away, without further threatening it.

4. Wear heavy gloves when working in weeds, firewood, etc. where snakes may be hidden. Dispose of garbage to prevent colonies of rodents from forming, which attract the snakes to the area.

SYMPTOMS EXPERIENCED WHEN BITTEN

1. The skin will be broken and fang marks will be present.

2. Pain and swelling at the site may develop rapidly and may be followed by a purple discoloration of the skin, bleeding at the site, nausea and vomiting.*

3. If the injury is severe, dizziness, shock, cramps, blindness or convulsions may also occur.

*The exception to number two above is the response to a bite from a Mohave Rattlesnake, in which no swelling, pain, or discoloration at the site will occur. The reason is that the venom primarily affects the nervous system. The other symptoms will be rapidly apparent and may include respiratory failure and coma.

FIRST-AID TREATMENT

First-aid is just that—it does not replace medical treatment in any way, and in fact, many forms of first aid can cause more harm. THE ONLY TREATMENT FOR A SNAKEBITE IS **ANTIVENOM (ANTIVENIN)** ADMINISTERED AT A HOSPITAL.

1. Sucking on the wound is only beneficial in the first 15 minutes. Cutting the wound does more damage, and should not be done.

2. Using ice may do more damage than good, since it further decreases circulation.

3. A tourniquet should not be used by non-medical personnel because it decreases circulation, and when the tourniquet is first tightened then released, the accumulated venom may flow rapidly into the circulation, causing physiological complications and possibly death.

The misconception of most persons bit by a venomous snake is that if the venom is either squeezed out, sucked out, or prevented from entering the circulation in some way, the person will be just fine. The truth is that the venom's main effect on the tissues does the most damage. This effect is swelling and decrease in circulation.

As the tissues break down and actually begin to die, the proteins released cause the entire body systems to fail and the person to eventually die. Venom in the circulation causes blood clotting changes, and internal hemorrhaging or excessive clotting can occur. Even a severe injury can be treated effectively if the victim is transported quickly to a hospital for treatment with antivenom.

Therefore, first aid needs to consist of rapid, safe transport, and keeping the person calm and resting to prevent more rapid progression of the venom. Every effort should be made to avoid further decreasing circulation of the injury site.

Keep in mind, that a victim who receives multiple bites, a child, an elderly or debilitated person, or in fact anyone may become extremely ill in a very short period of time and the rescuer must be prepared to perform CPR if necessary. Also, NEVER allow the victim to ingest alcohol or drugs to control the pain, since this will increase complications.

TREATMENT AT THE HOSPITAL

1. An IV (intravenous) line may be started, and the blood type of the victim may be determined in case a transfusion is needed. A skin test to determine sensitivity to the antivenom may be done.

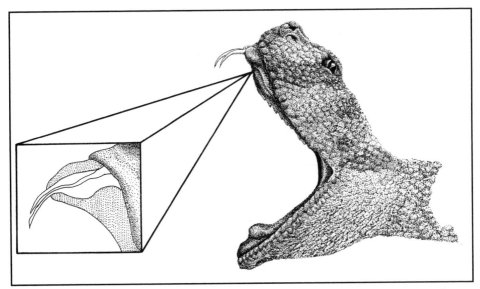

Pit Viper fangs are hollow and direct the flow of venom into prey. Some snakes have larger fangs than those depicted here. *(Illustration by Kirt M. Messick)*

2. Antibiotics and a tetanus injection may be given. Antivenom may be administered by IV over a period of several hours. Blood may be given to support the blood pressure if needed. Other medications may be given to control pain.

3. While the antivenom is being administered, the physician may enlarge the wound site to improve circulation or may use a constriction band to control the advancement of the swelling caused by the venom.

Remember, if you are bitten by ANY snake, and you don't know if it is venomous or not, it's best to assume it is and get medical assistance. Also remember, in the case of a Coral Snake or even a Mohave Rattlesnake, there will be little pain or swelling involved to indicate a severe bite and symptoms may not occur right away. But when they do, they can progress very rapidly.

Don't spend time capturing the snake, because the treatment is based on the symptoms experienced, not the species of snake. There is only one antivenom used for all the venomous snakes in our range, except for the Mohave Rattlesnake and Coral Snake, which have their own antivenoms. The physician need not see the snake to know which antivenom to use—simply give him a description, and he'll base his treatment on what the injury is, and how much damage has occurred.

If no symptoms occur, it means that the snake was either non-venomous or the venom did not successfully enter the tissues.

A victim who did not get injected with venom with the first bite, and decides to catch or kill the snake to take it with him is likely to get bitten again, this time with a full-blown injury. Furthermore, snakes can bite even after they are dead. Several cases of snakebite have occurred when a snake was decapitated and the head bit the person through reflexive opening and closing of the jaws.

In the following section, individual kinds of Pit Vipers of the Southwest are described. Most are the Rattlesnakes, which are identified by the presence of flat, dry tail segments that are vibrated by the snake to produce a buzzing noise that serves as a distraction to predators. Rattlesnakes grow a new segment each time they shed, and they periodically lose the outermost segments as well. So counting the rattles to determine age is not in any way accurate. Purposefully killing a Rattlesnake to hang the skin on the wall and boast about the "ancient rattlesnake you caught that has 28 rattles" probably won't get you the acclaim you seek.

COMMON NAME: **Trans-Pecos Copperhead**

SCIENTIFIC NAME: *Agkistrodon contortrix pictigaster*

IDENTIFICATION: This is the only subspecies of Copperhead Snake that is found in our range. They have a bulky body and dark, chestnut-brown or copper crossbands that are wide and separated by narrow, pale areas, making these snakes vivid in color, especially along the belly side.

HABITS: The vivid coloration of these snakes allows them to blend in very well with the leaf debris and rocky canyons near the waterways along which they reside. During the winter, these snakes will hibernate in communes with other snakes. Unfortunately, this makes them vulnerable to hunters who participate in roundups for sport. These activities, as well as the destruction of their natural environments, are taking a toll on the populations of the Copperheads, as well as the other Pit Vipers in our range. These snakes consume small rodents and large insects.

REPRODUCTION: Females give live birth to up to 12 young in midsummer.

RANGE: Big Bend region of west Texas.

Massasaugas are a group of tiny, "pigmy" Rattlesnakes. Although small, they have a potent venom.   *(Photograph by Erik Stoops)*

COMMON NAME: **Desert Massasauga**

SCIENTIFIC NAME: *Sistrurus catenatus edwardsii*

IDENTIFICATION: This is the only subspecies of Massasauga in our range. The 9 large scales on the top of the head identify it as different from the other Rattlesnakes. This subspecies is a faded gray with dark brown, rounded blotches. Adults are small, growing to a length of 18 to 30 inches, and are heavy-bodied with a stocky tail and a rattle.

HABITS: The Chippewa Indians gave this snake its name, which means "Great River Mouth," because they are commonly found in swampland or grassland areas near the mouths of rivers in the East as well as in desert grasslands in the West. On warm days they will come out in daylight to sun themselves, but in the hot summer months are most active at night. They consume frogs, lizards, and small rodents.

REPRODUCTION: In late summer, females give live birth to up to 12 young, which are 6 to 8 inches long.

RANGE: Texas, New Mexico, and extreme SE Arizona.

RELATED SPECIES:

> Western Pigmy Rattlesnake *(Sistrurus miliarius streckeri)*
> Features: Length 15 to 28 inches—tiny rattle on tail only heard a few feet away. Found in East Texas.

Mohave Rattlesnakes are unique in the fact that their venom primarily affects the nervous system of their prey. *(Photograph by Jeffrey Howland)*

COMMON NAME: **Mohave Rattlesnake**

SCIENTIFIC NAME: *Crotalus scutulatus*

IDENTIFICATION: Color is grayish-green, olive, or greenish-brown, possibly with yellow. They have brown diamond-shaped blotches bordered in white down the midline of the back. Rings on the tail are black and white, the white rings are larger. Adults are approximately 3 feet.

HABITS: They inhabit open desert areas and can be found crossing a road or in a dry riverbed out in the open in the morning or evening. They find shelter from the desert heat during the day. The venom of the Mohave Rattlesnake is unique compared to the other southwestern Crotalines, since it is highly neurotoxic—causing death of prey by paralysis much like the Coral Snake. A specific antivenom has been made to treat the victims who receive bites from these snakes. These snakes hunt in the Joshua Tree forests and in groves of brush and cacti for the rodents they consume.

REPRODUCTION: Females give live birth to up to 10 young in late summer.

RANGE: Nevada, California, Arizona, and southwest New Mexico.

This young Mohave Rattlesnake is more brightly marked than an adult. Despite its youth, it has a potent venom. *(Photograph by Jeffrey Howland)*

COMMON NAME: **Sidewinder**

SCIENTIFIC NAME: *Crotalus cerastes*

IDENTIFICATION: These snakes are pale gray, tan, or even pinkish-gray. They often match the color of the surrounding soil in the area they are found. They have rough scales and are patterned with small brown or gray blotches along the back and sides. They are identified by the presence of a triangular "horn" over each eye.

HABITS: Another form of identification is possible by observing their unique form of movement. A Sidewinder moves its body by thrusting its looped body forward and to the side of the head, then moving the head forward, and then repeating this motion. In the sand, J-shaped marks will be observed after a Sidewinder has moved. This form of locomotion is essential to allow these snakes to move rapidly on the loose sand in the desert environment that they inhabit. They consume small rodents and lizards.

REPRODUCTION: Females give live birth to litters of up to 15 young in the fall.

RANGE: Southern Utah and Nevada, California, and Arizona.

Sidewinders look much like other Rattlesnakes, but have a horn over each eye, and move in a different manner. *(Photograph by Jeffrey Howland)*

Sidewinders blend in well to the surrounding desert sands because their color usually matches their environment. *(Photograph by Jeffrey Howland)*

Snakes and other Reptiles of the Southwest

**The following color photographs are presented
in the same order as they appear in the text.**

Note: Even though color photographs assist us in identifying reptiles,
some of them are still difficult to see, as they have been photographed
in their natural environment where the ability to blend in with their
surroundings is an important factor for survival.

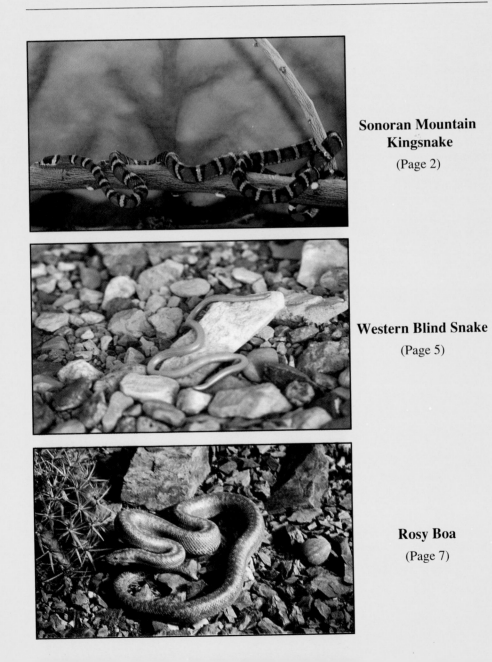

**Sonoran Mountain
Kingsnake**

(Page 2)

Western Blind Snake

(Page 5)

Rosy Boa

(Page 7)

**Western Terrestrial
Garter Snake**

(Page 9)

**Black-Necked
Garter Snake**

(Page 10)

Ground Snake

(Page 12)

Glossy Snake

(Page 13)

Longnose Snake
(Page 16)

Shovelnose Snake
(Page 17)

**Big Bend
Patchnose Snake**
(Page 18)

**Mountain
Patchnose Snake**
(Page 19)

Gopher Snake

(Page 20)

San Diego Gopher Snake

(Page 21)

Trans-Pecos Rat Snake

(Page 22)

Desert Kingsnake

(Page 23)

Baja Mountain Kingsnake

(Page 24)

Milk Snake

(Page 25)

Night Snake

(Page 27)

Coral Snake

(Page 30)

Pit Viper

(Page 31)

**Western
Diamondback
Rattlesnake**

(Page 32)

Massasauga

(Page 37)

Mohave Rattlesnake

(Page 38)

Mohave Rattlesnake
(Page 39)

Sidewinder
(Page 40)

Sidewinder
(Page 40)

**Red Diamond
Rattlesnake**
(Page 42)

Rock Rattlesnake
(Page 43)

**Banded Rock
Rattlesnake**
(Page 43)

Speckled Rattlesnake
(Page 44)

Blacktail Rattlesnake
(Page 45)

Western Rattlesnake
(Page 49)

**Southern Pacific
Rattlesnake**
(Page 49)

Softshell Turtle
(Page 52)

Softshell Turtle
(Page 55)

Desert Tortoise

(Page 56)

Desert Tortoise

(Page 57)

Desert Tortoise

(Page 58)

Collared Lizard

(Page 60)

**Lesser Earless
Lizard**

(Page 61)

**Western Banded
Gecko**

(Page 63)

**Granite Night
Lizard**

(Page 65)

**Desert Night
Lizard**

(Page 66)

Texas Alligator Lizard

(Page 69)

Gila Monster

(Page 72)

Gila Monster

(Page 74)

Whiptail Lizard

(Page 77)

Gilbert's Skink
(Page 79)

Collared Lizards
(Page 82)

Collared Lizard
(Page 83)

**Zebratail
Lizard**
(Page 84)

**Greater Earless
Lizard**

(Page 84)

**Lesser Earless
Lizard**

(Page 85)

**Side-Blotched
Lizard**

(Page 86)

Desert Iguana

(Page 87)

Desert Iguana
(Page 88)

Leopard Lizard
(Page 88)

**Fringe-Toed
Lizard**
(Page 90)

Tree Lizard
(Page 91)

Short Horned Lizard

(Page 93)

Coast Horned Lizard

(Page 94)

Flat-tail Horned Lizard

(Page 94)

Yarrow's Spiny Lizard

(Page 96)

COMMON NAME: **Western Diamondback Rattlesnake**

SCIENTIFIC NAME: *Crotalus atrox*

IDENTIFICATION: A large, heavy-bodied snake; adults can reach lengths of 6 feet. The head is large and distinct. Color is gray, brown, or with hints of pink or yellow with dark diamond- or hexagon-shaped blotches. The tail is ringed with black and white bands (coon-tail).

HABITS: These snakes have a tendency to reside near human populations, most likely attracted by the population of rodents that are also attracted to our cities. In fact, these snakes are secretive, and a den of large numbers of these and other hibernating snakes may be present and not be noticed by the humans residing in that area. Although secretive and nocturnal, these snakes will stand their ground in defense of themselves, especially if they have no opportunity to escape. They will raise their head and the front of their body off the ground in preparation of a defensive strike after they rattle loudly in warning.

REPRODUCTION: Females give live birth to up to 24 young in late summer.

RANGE: Flat, open desert areas and dry riverbeds of California, Arizona, New Mexico, and Texas.

Refer to photo on page 32.

COMMON NAME: **Red Diamond Rattlesnake**

SCIENTIFIC NAME: *Crotalus ruber*

IDENTIFICATION: A very stout Rattlesnake that is brick-red, reddish-tan, or even pink in color and has blotches along the back that are diamond-shaped. The tail is ringed with black and white bands. Also called the California Diamond-back.

HABITS: These snakes hunt at night for squirrels, rodents, and birds in the cooler coastal areas as well as the mountainous foothills of the desert where they reside. They find shelter during the day under a rocky outcropping or dense brush. Although large, growing to an average length of 3 feet, they are relatively docile and are often resistant to using their rattle or striking, even when pressed. Although they prefer to escape, if they feel threatened enough and are not given the chance to escape, they can and will strike.

REPRODUCTION: Females give live birth to up to 15 young in late summer.

RANGE: Southern and Baja California.

Red Diamond Rattlesnakes resemble Western Diamondbacks, but are reddish in color and found only in California. *(Photograph by Jeffrey Howland)*

COMMON NAME: **Rock Rattlesnake**

SCIENTIFIC NAME: *Crotalus lepidus*

IDENTIFICATION: A slender Rattlesnake that is grayish-blue or gray-green with tan or pink underneath and has irregular-shaped brown or black crossbands on the body. The Mottled form has spotting between the bands, and the Banded form has very distinct crossbands.

HABITS: These snakes reside in areas heavily strewn with rocks and boulders, and their pattern effectively camouflages them from easy sight. During the day, they bask on the rocks and hunt for lizards, small snakes, and small rodents once they are warm. Because they are difficult to spot, persons hiking in rocky areas must be cautious. It is very easy to place your hands or foot on one when reaching for a hand or foothold. Always look where you plan to place your hands and feet before moving.

REPRODUCTION: Up to 8 young are born during the summer.

RANGE: Southeast Arizona, New Mexico, and Texas.

Rock Rattlesnakes are very much at home in areas with rocky crevices and boulders. (Photograph by Jeffrey Howland)

The Banded Rock Rattlesnake has distinct bands and a speckled background that camouflages him in rocky areas. (Photograph by Shay Hamper)

Speckled Rattlesnakes in their natural environment can be easily overlooked if one is not alert and observant. *(Photograph by Shay Hamper)*

COMMON NAME: **Speckled Rattlesnake**

SCIENTIFIC NAME: *Crotalus mitchellii*

IDENTIFICATION: Adults grow to an average length of 3 feet. They have a marbled or speckled appearance that resembles the color of the rocks in the area they are found. Color may be tan, brown, yellow, pink, or reddish with faint blotches or crossbands made up of small dots in clusters.

HABITS: WATCH YOUR STEP! These snakes blend in with their surroundings extremely well and can be easily overlooked. They are active in warm weather during the day and at night when the temperature is hot. They eat a variety of small rodents, lizards, and birds. They reside around rocky outcroppings in canyons and in any areas with large boulders or rock piles in the cooler desert or mountain foothills.

REPRODUCTION: Females give live birth to up to 11 young in late summer.

RANGE: Southern Utah, Nevada, and California, and western Arizona.

Blacktail Rattlesnakes, as their name suggests, are identified by the presence of a black tail, but not black rattles.   *(Photograph by Tom Wright)*

COMMON NAME: **Blacktail Rattlesnake**

SCIENTIFIC NAME: *Crotalus molossus*

IDENTIFICATION: Grayish-green or yellowish with irregular crossbands that are darker than the background color and bordered in white or yellow. Scales are rough, and each scale is a solid color. The tail is dark black and contrasts with the body.

HABITS: This is a secretive snake that is considered docile because of its reluctance to aggressively defend itself. However, it is still venomous and potentially dangerous. It can be seen basking in the sun in moderately warm weather in rocky areas of the mountains and canyons and in dry riverbed washes. Consumes small rodents, and hunts primarily at night.

REPRODUCTION: Females give live birth to approximately 5 young in summer.

RANGE: Arizona, New Mexico, and Texas.

COMMON NAME: **Twin-Spotted Rattlesnake**

SCIENTIFIC NAME: *Crotalus pricei*

IDENTIFICATION: A slender snake with a background color of tan or silver-gray. Has two rows of identifying round brown or reddish spots along the back. They grow to an average length of 1 1/2 feet.

HABITS: This snake is small in size, and its small rattle can only be heard a few yards away and resembles the sound made by a cicada (locust). Suns itself on the rocks during the day. It is shy and quick to hide if danger approaches. These snakes eat lizards and small mammals. In the higher elevations they reside in mountainous areas in pine woodlands near rocks. These snakes are not commonly found, and reside only in a limited area in our range.

REPRODUCTION: Females give live birth to 2 to 7 young in late summer.

RANGE: Southeastern Arizona into Mexico.

COMMON NAME: **Tiger Rattlesnake**

SCIENTIFIC NAME: *Crotalus tigris*

IDENTIFICATION: Background color may be tan, pinkish-gray or even light lavender with multiple darker gray or brown crossbands resembling tiger stripes that have a marbled appearance. Tiger Rattlesnakes are often confused with the Speckled Rattlesnakes, but they are smaller, growing to a length of 2 to 3 feet. Also, the head is small, and the rattle is large in proportion to the rest o the body.

HABITS: These snakes are found amid rocky outcroppings and in canyons associated with heavy groves of brush and cacti. They are active both day and night, most likely more nocturnal during the summer months, and have even been seen crossing roads after evening showers. They consume lizards and small mammals. They are not a common snake and are only infrequently seen in a limited area.

REPRODUCTION: Females give live birth to up to 8 young.

RANGE: South-central Arizona, especially around the Tucson Mountain Preserves.

COMMON NAME: **Ridgenose Rattlesnake**

SCIENTIFIC NAME: *Crotalus willardi*

IDENTIFICATION: This is a small snake, growing to a length of only 1.5 to 2 feet. They may be light brown, reddish, or light gray with narrow light-colored crossbands, bordered with slightly darker coloration. Depending on the subspecies, they may have white flash marks on the side of the face. Identified by the presence of a ridge along the edge of the snout.

HABITS: The general coloration will vary depending on the location of the snake, since they usually match the color of the leaf debris found on the floor of the woodlands where they reside. They are shy snakes and may spend the day basking in the sun or hunting for the lizards and small rodents they consume. They are a woodland snake and are often found near water and, in fact, become more active after a rain storm in warm weather. These snakes are protected by the Government, especially in Arizona, because of their risk for total elimination. They are limited to a very small area in Arizona and New Mexico.

COMMON NAME: **Western Rattlesnake**

SCIENTIFIC NAME: *Crotalus viridis*

IDENTIFICATION: There are several subspecies of the Western Rattlesnake found in our range, all with a wide variety of colors. The pattern is usually made up of brown blotches bordered with either a darker or lighter color. Blotches may be roughly round or diamond-shaped and become faded as they progress towards the tail.

HABITS: Found in a variety of habitats, depending on the subspecies; often found around rocks and brush as well as woodland areas. They are relatively excitable and can be aggressive if they feel the need to defend themselves. In areas where caves or underground caverns are located and particularly in higher elevations, these snakes may hibernate in large groups in "dens," possibly with non-venomous snakes as well. Active during the day in warm weather and nocturnal in the hot summer months, these snakes hunt for small mammals and lizards.

REPRODUCTION: Females give live birth to up to 20 young, depending on the subspecies, usually in the fall.

RANGE: Variable; depending on subspecies. Some subspecies are located in a limited range and are only rarely encountered.

SUBSPECIES:

Grand Canyon Rattlesnake *(Crotalus viridis abyssus)*
Range: Grand Canyon National Park, Arizona.
Features: Background reddish-brown. Protected by the Park.

Arizona Black Rattlesnake *(Crotalus viridis cerberus)*
Range: Central Arizona and western New Mexico.
Features: Dark brown or black with faint blotches bordered with white. Young snakes are obviously blotched.

Midget Faded Rattlesnake *(Crotalus viridis concolor)*
Range: Includes limited areas in western Colorado and eastern Utah.
Features: Background color light yellow with or without blotches. Rarely seen in our range.

Southern Pacific Rattlesnake *(Crotalus viridis helleri)*
Range: Southern and Baja California.
Features: Has diamond-shaped blotches and resembles the Arizona Black Rattlesnake.

Great Basin Rattlesnake *(Crotalus viridis lutosus)*
Range: Includes California, Nevada, Arizona, and Utah.
Features: Blotches resemble narrow bands.

Hopi Rattlesnake *(Crotalus viridis nuntius)*
Range: Northern Arizona, Hopi Indian Reservation.
Features: Background color reddish-brown or pinkish-tan. Rarely seen; small range of occurrence.

Northern Pacific Rattlesnake (Crotalus viridis oreganus)
Range: Includes California.
Features: Resembles the Southern Pacific Rattlesnake, but has distinct rings on the tail.

Western Rattlesnakes are plentiful in the Southwest, and there are a number of subspecies, each with slightly different coloring. *(Photograph by Jeffrey Howland)*

This Southern Pacific Rattlesnake is one of the darkest subspecies of the Western Rattlesnake found in our range. *(Photograph by Jeffrey Howland)*

TURTLES and TORTOISES

*Illustration by
James Richmond*

Turtles and tortoises are classified separately, although they have similar body structures. Turtles are classified under the scientific order TESTUDINE, and the tortoises under the family TESTUDINIDAE. Turtles are primarily considered to be those forms that dwell in or near water, and tortoises the land-dwelling forms. The term "Chelonian" is often used to describe turtles, especially those associated with water, and is derived from the scientific name of the Green Sea Turtle. In the following pages, when the word turtle is used, it also refers to tortoises, unless otherwise noted.

First, a little family history: Turtles that are seen today have changed very little in the past 170 million or more years. This means that they were already in existence when the dinosaurs were around and have stuck around ever since. This is easy to understand when you consider the characteristics of a turtle's body. They are well prepared for the lives they live, no matter how bad the weather gets!

The turtle's body is unique in the fact that it has a shell. The upper shell, or **carapace**, is made up of hardened shields, that are actually hardened layers of skin, just like the scales of the lizards and snakes.

Underneath these shields are plates that are made of bone. These are fused together and cover the entire body. Both the upper shell and the lower shell, called the **plastron** serve to protect the turtle from injury and are essentially the backbone and ribs of the turtle. The carapace and the plastron are joined together at the sides, which leaves openings for the head, tail and limbs. The pattern of shields that make up the shell are used by scientists to distinguish the different types of turtles, which amount to over 200. Different turtles have different kinds of limbs as well. The land turtles, or tortoises, have a club-like foot with short claws. The fresh-water turtles have small, webbed feet with longer claws, or they may have flipper-like feet, much like the Sea Turtles. The neck of a turtle may be short or extremely long and can usually be pulled back under the shell for protection.

Turtles do not have teeth. But they do have hard beaks and powerful jaws. These beaks may be quite roughened, resembling teeth. Turtles have an outer ear structure, and are also able to hear sounds carried through the air by picking up vibrations through the body and shell. Turtles have excellent eyesight and are able to distinguish different colors.

Have you ever wondered how a turtle can breathe with this hard, confining shell compressing its body? There are two ways this is accomplished.

First, turtles may actually swallow air and force it into their lungs. A second way is by stretching the neck and shoulders forward and the hips backwards thus filling the lungs by expanding and contracting the body. Actually their lungs are so large and turtles use so little oxygen that they really don't have to breathe very often at all. Many spend hours and even days under the water without having to come up for air, especially during the cooler months when they are hibernating.

Like all reptiles, turtles are cold-blooded, and in the cooler months they conserve energy by hibernation. They become active again when the weather warms. Because their bodies don't expend a lot of energy keeping a constant body temperature and they're fairly inactive at any time, they can survive with little food. Turtles eat a variety of plant material, insects, and water-dwelling creatures including fish.

It takes a lot of effort for turtles to move from one place to another. Their limbs extend awkwardly out at right angles to their body, and they are permanently burdened by the relatively heavy weight of their shell. This less than sleek design makes sitting around all day about the only choice they have. They bask in the sun, eat a few plants and insects here and there, and when the time is right, find a mate and produce offspring. Add to this the fact that they sleep all winter, and don't have to run from their enemies, and you can see they lead a pretty comfortable life!

There is one stage of a turtle's life that is an exception to its easy-going existence and is full of danger—the stage of infancy. After a male and female turtle mate (or male and female tortoise—they don't mix), the female prepares a shallow hole in which she lays her eggs. She covers the leathery eggs with dirt or leaves and leaves them to incubate on their own. The tiny babies that eventually hatch have soft delicate shells and have no means to defend themselves, so they are at great risk of being eaten by other animals. Those young turtles who do escape and are able to hide may go many months without food, since they can't afford to come out into the open to hunt. The first year is the worst; after that, the shell has become large enough and tough enough to protect them from harm.

The following pages describe several kinds of turtles native to the southwestern United States. The features discussed as a means of identification will vary somewhat within the species.

This Softshell turtle has a flexible carapace, webbed feet, and a pointed snout, which helps to identify it.

(Photograph by Tom Wright)

COMMON NAME: **Western Pond Turtle**

SCIENTIFIC NAME: *Clemmys marmorata*

IDENTIFICATION: Plastron is usually pale yellow. The carapace is dark brown or black, and some specimens have black blotches and possibly yellow streaks as well. The adult's carapace can grow to a length of 6 to 7 inches.

HABITS: This is a freshwater, mostly aquatic turtle. Although a good swimmer, it spends much of its time sitting on logs or dense vegetation in small ponds, marshes, streams, and even irrigation ditches and canals. They are quite shy, but will defend themselves by biting if they feel threatened. They feed on small worms and minnows.

REPRODUCTION: The males have a concave plastron. Females lay approximately 2 to 10 eggs in April to August in sandy, marshy areas. Neonates (babies) emerge about 12 weeks later and find immediate shelter.

RANGE: They are found in Sierra Nevada through Baja California as well as in isolated populations in western Nevada.

COMMON NAME: **Yellow Mud Turtle**

SCIENTIFIC NAME: *Kinosternon flavescens*

IDENTIFICATION: The plastron of the mud turtles in general is unique in that there are two flexible lobes, one in the front and one in the back, that can be closed over the opening of the head and tail after they are withdrawn inside. This particular species has this characteristic and a smooth, brown or olive-gray carapace with a yellow or brown plastron. The shell can grow to a length of 4 to 6 inches.

HABITS: When molested, these turtles release a foul odor. These turtles are often found in groups near ponds, water holes, and drainage ditches. They feed on most kinds of animal foods—insects, worms, snails, minnows, and even refuse and dead animals.

REPRODUCTION: They mate in May through September. The females lay anywhere from 1 to 6 eggs, and the neonates emerge approximately 10 weeks later.

RANGE: They range from desert areas to the forest and mountain areas up to elevations of 7,000 feet in southeast New Mexico, Arizona, and Texas.

RELATED SPECIES:

Mexican Mud Turtle *(Kinosternon hirtipes)*
Sonoran Mud Turtle *(Kinosternon sonoriense)*

COMMON NAME: **Western Box Turtle**

SCIENTIFIC NAME: *Terrapene ornata*

IDENTIFICATION: Box Turtles have a unique appearance in that they have a high domed carapace and a hinged plastron that can be tightly closed over the head as a defense measure. The Western Box Turtle is brown, reddish-brown, or black with a pattern of many yellow lines. The shell measures 4 to 5 inches in an adult.

HABITS: Another unique feature is that this turtle spends most, if not all, of its life on land. These turtles are often confused for tortoises for this reason. They typically live in grasslands, open forests, or desert brushlands, but are usually within range of some sort of water source. They are active during the rainy seasonand will often be seen crossing roads in the early morning hours. They feed on small insects, worms, and vegetation, and they can adapt very well to living in an enclosed backyard.

REPRODUCTION: Males often have red eyes, and the females have yellowish-brown eyes. Females lay 3 to 7 eggs in soft forest debris or sand, and incubation takes approximately 10 weeks.

RANGE: Texas, southern Arizona and into Mexico.

COMMON NAME: Spiny Softshell Turtle

SCIENTIFIC NAME: *Apalone spinifera*

IDENTIFICATION: Softshell Turtles are in a family of their own: the Trionychidea. They feature soft, flat, flexible, leathery shells, long necks, and pointed snouts. The Spiny Softshell Turtle, native to the Southwest, may be olive-green or gray with yellow or black spots on the flat carapace, with a white or cream-colored plastron that is equally soft and flexible. The feet are webbed and paddle-like.

HABITS: They primarily live in water, but will occasionally bask in the mud along the banks of creeks, ponds, lakes, and canals. They are able to burrow into the bottom soils of these waterways, and remain there for long periods of time, stretching only their necks upward to take an occasional breath of air. They are fast swimmers, even surprisingly fast on land, and difficult to approach. They produce a painful bite when handled.

REPRODUCTION: Females lay 4 to 30 eggs in the soil near the banks of the waterways, and this species may reproduce twice in one year. Males grow to be 10 inches, females 18 inches.

RANGE: Arizona, Utah, Nevada, Texas, and western California.

Softshell Turtles are usually found submerged under water, where they are able to stay for long periods of time.   *(Photograph by Tom Wright)*

COMMON NAME: Desert Tortoise

SCIENTIFIC NAME: *Gopherus agassizii*

IDENTIFICATION: Tortoises, being land-dwelling turtles, have been placed into the family **Testudinidae**, with the Desert Tortoise being one of four Tortoises found in North America. Desert Tortoises are brown or reddish-brown with a high-domed carapace and large, clubbed limbs that are completely without webbing. They may have lighter colored spots or blotches on their shell, and they can grow to a length of 10 to 14 inches.

HABITS: They are essentially the same as the Gopher Tortoise native to the eastern United States. They are adept at digging burrows in soft earth, in which they will hibernate during the winter and find shelter from the extreme desert heat during the summer. The Desert Tortoise can drink up to 40 percent of its weight in water and conserve it for when water is scarce. They reach full maturity after 20 years and can live up to 100 years.

REPRODUCTION: Males often have a slightly concave plastron. Females lay 1 to 15 eggs in funnel-shaped holes or burrows, and the neonates emerge approximately 3 months later.

The high-domed carapace and clubbed feet are characteristic of all Gopher Tortoises, such as the Desert Tortoise seen here. (Photograph by Jeffrey Howland)

HABITAT AND RANGE: Desert Tortoises are found in places such as dry riverbeds in the desert as well as brushland and grassland areas and cactus fields in Arizona, southeastern California, southern Nevada, and southwest Utah.

RELATED SPECIES: Berlandier's Tortoise, also called the Texas Tortoise *(Gopherus berlandieri)*

OTHER INFORMATION: The Desert Tortoise Mohave population found northwest of the Colorado River is under Government protection because of its potential to become extinct in the wild. Drastic reduction in Desert Tortoise numbers has been caused by disease, habitat destruction, decreased food availability, injury from off road vehicles and livestock, and over-collection. People should make no attempt to capture specimens, since it constitutes an illegal act, and no attempt should be made to handle any wild Desert Tortoise in any way. Desert Tortoises also suffer from vitamin deficiencies, because the proper plants that supply their needs have been replaced by "foreign" types of vegetation that have less nutritional value.

If a Desert Tortoise is found in a developed area, make no attempt to pick it up or handle it in any way. Call the local Wildlife Agency and inform them of the location, so that attempts can be made to safely move the tortoise. If contact is made; that is, if one is found in a neighborhood or backyard, make no attempt to take it out to the desert. Instead, call the local Game and Fish Department or State Wildlife Agency for instructions.

Desert Tortoises dig burrows in soft earth in order to create a place to escape from the heat of the sun. *(Photograph by Jeffrey Howland)*

The natural populations of the Desert Tortoise have dwindled alarmingly due to the spread of disease and habitat destruction.   *(Photograph by Jeffrey Howland)*

LIZARDS

The lizards and snakes are joined under the order of SQUAMATA, which refers to the fact that these reptiles have scales. The lizards, placed under the suborder of SAURIA or LACERTILIA, are quite similar to the snakes in many aspects. It is not correct to assume that lizards are lizards because they have legs and eyelids and snakes do not, because there are exceptions to this. There is such a thing as a legless lizard.

All lizards have an outer skin that is made up of a particular pattern of tough, dry scales. Lizards shed their outer layer of skin regularly (referred to as molting). The new skin that develops may change pattern slightly with each molt as the lizard grows. Unlike snakes, which usually shed in one piece, lizards molt as if they were peeling from a severe sunburn.

Lizards usually have good eyesight, and they depend on this in order to successfully catch the insects they regularly consume. Most lizards have eyelids that open and shut much like ours do. But again, there are those exceptions which do not have eyelids; these have a scale, or "spectacle," over the eye which protects it. Some lizards even have a clear area on their lower eyelid that allows them to see with their eyes closed. Lizards have many small, sharp teeth that grow along the inner surfaces of the upper and lower jaw. They chew their food somewhat before swallowing it.

Some lizards have long, forked tongues, while others have thick, short tongues, and still some have no tongues at all. The tongue of a lizard is used to "smell" the air, as with snakes, and is also used in eating.

One of the ways scientists previously used to tell the difference between a snake and a lizard was the presence of a visible eardrum in a lizard that is usually located behind the eye on both sides of the head. Unfortunately, scientists found out that there are even exceptions to this, since there are a few lizards that do not have this feature.

Most lizards have forward and hind limbs. The hind limbs are larger. Each limb has four or five fingers or toes. There are a few lizards that do not have limbs and are thus classified as Legless Lizards.

Most lizards, like this Collared Lizard spend a large portion of the day basking in the sun for warmth. *(Photograph by Tom Wright)*

All lizards have a tail that is essential to them in one way or another. The tail helps them balance themselves, and in some species, the tail is used to grasp branches and other objects for support when climbing. Some species store large quantities of fat in their tails for use during periods of hibernation. Some lizards have large, muscular tails that they use to defend themselves by thrashing at the enemy. As important as the tail is to a lizard, losing it can also be an advantage. Some lizards can rid themselves of their tail very easily in order to escape the clutches of a predator.

Most lizards that readily lose their tails can also regenerate them, or grow them back. Of course, not all lizards can grow a tail back, and those that cannot are not eager to lose the ones they have. In fact, some lizards may die from an injured or severed tail, especially those which use them to store fat for hibernation.

The behavior and mannerisms of lizards are one of their most interesting features. Most lizards are active, and spend a large amount of time hunting, courting, mating, and defending their territory, which burns up most of the calories they take in. Lizards spend the morning and early afternoon hours warming in the sun. In the fierce heat of the day, they must find shelter from the sun in order to survive. In the winter, lizards hibernate like other reptiles.

This Lesser Earless Lizard has warmed itself by basking on a rock, and is now alert and ready to hunt. *(Photograph by Jeffrey Howland)*

Many lizards protect themselves by always being alert and by running very quickly for shelter when they perceive a threat. Their natural coloration camouflages and allows them to blend into the surrounding rocks and vegetation. Some lizards, such as Chameleons, can change their skin color to match their environment.

In the southwestern United States, lizards of many kinds are abundant and vary in coloring and pattern. The following pages are dedicated to describing the different groups of lizards and provide examples of each group or family.

GECKOS

Family Gekkonidae

In general, the Geckos are a family of lizards with several unique character-istics. They usually have a somewhat flattened appearance and short limbs. Many species have small toe pads which act like Velcro®, that enable them to climb vertically or even upside down.

Most Geckos do not have moveable eyelids, but instead have a clear scale, or spectacle over their eyes that protect them. An exception to this is the Geckos of the genus *Coleonyx*, which include the Banded Geckos native to the Southwest, that have eyelids.

Geckos in general are seemingly fragile with skin that is soft and tears easily. They release their tails quickly when caught, and regenerate them.

One unusual feature of Geckos is their voice. They are able to vocalize in some fashion, usually in the form of chirps or squeaks when defending them-selves.

The Tokay Gecko (*Gekko gecko*) of southeast Asia is an exotic Gecko that is commonly seen in pet stores, and is one of the largest Gecko known, as well as one of the loudest. Geckos are insect eaters and thus are popular in many parts of the world,. They are even commonly invited or introduced into the home to provide pest control for the home owners. It is not at all uncommon to find Geckos in garages, patios, or even inside the home clinging to the walls in search of insects.

COMMON NAME: **Western Banded Gecko**

SCIENTIFIC NAME: *Coleonyx variegatus*

IDENTIFICATION: This lizard grows to an adult length of 6 inches. They have eyelids that protrude somewhat and may even appear to have "eyelashes." They are light tan, yellow, or pinkish in appearance with loose, supple skin. They have dark brown or black, band-like blotches as well as spots that are extremely distinct in juveniles. The original tail is usually ringed. But since most lose their first tail at one stage or another, these rings will usually be absent; regenerated tails are plainly colored. The toes are slender without pads.

HABITS: When caught, these lizards will chirp or squeal. They feed on small insects, primarily hunt in the early morning hours and at night, and find protection from the heat during the day. They typically hide under logs, rocks, and under trash heaps in canyons, open desert, vacant lots, and backyards.

Western Banded Geckos are slender lizards with soft pastel skin colors that help them blend into their surroundings.   *(Photograph by Jeffrey Howland)*

REPRODUCTION: Mating occurs in the spring. One to 3 eggs are deposited by the female under rocks. Neonates emerge in approximately 30 to 40 days and are approximately 1 inch long.

RANGE: California, Nevada, Utah, and Arizona.

RELATED SPECIES:

> Texas Banded Gecko *(Coleonyx brevis)*
> Range: New Mexico, Texas, and Mexico.
> Features: Eyelids white-rimmed. Generally smaller in size. Fully
>> nocturnal.

> Reticulated Gecko *(Coleonyx reticulatus)*
> Range: Extreme southwest Texas.
> Features: Of limited range; rare. Skin with small tubercles. Nocturnal;
>> emerges after heavy rains.

COMMON NAME: **Leaf-Toed Gecko**

SCIENTIFIC NAME: *Phyllodactylus xanti*

IDENTIFICATION: Grows to a length of 3 to 4 inches. Has no eyelids, but instead has a transparent scale covering both eyes. May be pink or gray with or without dark brown blotches. Has tubercles along the back that are wart-like in appearance. This gecko is named for the two enlarged leaf-like pads located on the tips of the toes.

HABITS: These geckos will produce a squeak-like voice when startled or touched. They are nocturnal and come out after dark to search for the small, soft-bodied insects they eat. They are commonly found in backyards, open fields, and rocky outcroppings and frequently hide in the cracks and crevices of rocks, fallen cacti, and logs.

REPRODUCTION: Females lay 1 to 2 eggs in the spring, and the neonates emerge 30 to 40 days later.

RANGE: Desert areas in Baja California as well as the small islands in the Gulf of California.

NIGHT LIZARDS

Family Xantusiidae

In many ways, the Night Lizards are similar to the Geckos, having a generally flattened appearance as well as soft, supple skin along the body. They do not have moveable eyelids.

Although similar in many ways, the Night Lizards have several important differences from the Geckos that help to identify them. All Night Lizards have accurate vision at night, when they are most active.

The Night Lizards have small, round scales along the back that give them a roughened appearance, although the skin is actually quite soft to the touch. The scales along the bottom of the body are rectangular and larger than those along the top of the body. The head scales are also quite enlarged.

The Night Lizards do not have toe pads; instead each toe ends with a sharp claw, which assists these lizards in climbing the rocks and fallen tree trunks they inhabit.

Another major difference between a Gecko and a Night Lizard is in the manner in which the females give birth. Neonates are not hatched from eggs, but are born live and tail first after developing for several months within the female's body.

Night Lizards, as their name suggests, are fully nocturnal and have extremely light-sensitive eyes. They spend the day hiding, avoiding the heat and light of the sun, and emerge at night to hunt for insects.

Granite Night Lizards have a pattern of larger dark spots during the day that diminish in size at night. *(Photograph by Jeffrey Howland)*

COMMON NAME: **Granite Night Lizard**

SCIENTIFIC NAME: *Xantusia henshawi*

IDENTIFICATION: Like all Night Lizards, they have a flat body with soft skin that is made up of small, round scales on top and large, smooth scales underneath. They have a light-colored background with dark brown or black blotches that are larger during the day, and more like spots or speckles during the night hours. Adults reach a length of 4 to 6 inches.

HABITS: These lizards are active at night, hunting for the small insects they consume. They are very secretive and difficult to find. During the day, they will hide under fallen cacti, in rock crevices, and especially under granite slabs.

REPRODUCTION: Females give live birth to 1 or 2 young in August or September.

RANGE: Arid and semi-arid regions of southern and Baja California.

RELATED SPECIES:

> Island Night Lizard *(Klauberina riversiana)*
> Features: These grow to a length of 8 inches and are generally darker in color. They are an Endangered Species and are found only in the islands off of Southern California.

Unlike their relatives, Desert Night Lizards can be found hunting for insects both day and night. *(Photograph by Jeffrey Howland)*

COMMON NAME: **Desert Night Lizard**

SCIENTIFIC NAME: *Xantusia vigilis*

IDENTIFICATION: The color pattern varies among the different subspecies found in their range. In general, they may be olive, yellow, brown, or orange with a variable pattern comprised of many dark spots. The upper scales are small, smooth, and square. They grow to a length of 3 to 5 inches.

HABITS: Desert Night Lizards are not completely nocturnal as are the other Night Lizards. They hunt during early morning, late afternoon, and after dusk for the ants, beetles, flies, and termites they consume. They hide during the heat of the day under granite rock outcroppings and fallen yucca, agave, and Joshua trees. Their tails break off easily as an escape measure.

REPRODUCTION: Females give live birth to 1 to 3 young, in September and October.

RANGE: Nevada, Utah, Arizona, and California with a localized population in southwest Arizona.

ALLIGATOR LIZARDS

Family Anguidae

Alligator Lizards are one member of the family Anguidae, which are known for their long, shiny bodies and tails that are stiff due to the presence of a bony armor. Because of this stiffness, many would be unable to breathe were it not for the presence of a groove lengthwise along the sides of the body that allows chest expansion to occur.

These lizards have moveable eyelids and external ear openings, from which they see and hear quite well. They have extremely tiny legs and toes, and some species have no limbs at all.

Alligator lizards are adept at losing their tails when caught, and when the tail separates, it continues to writhe and move naturally for several minutes, while the lizard continues on its way. Other defense measures used by these lizards include fleeing, biting, or eliminating excrement in order to distract or deter the enemy. Other related species of Anguids that are legless and have tails over half the length of the body may also separate from the tails in times of danger. The lizard appears as if it has broken in half. This escape mechanism is responsible for many stories of folklore regarding these reptiles' ability to regenerate.

Alligator Lizards are carnivores and will readily consume insects and other lizards and mammals as well.

COMMON NAME: **Northern Alligator Lizard**

SCIENTIFIC NAME: *Elgaria coerulea*

IDENTIFICATION: This species of Alligator Lizard grows to an adult length of 8 to 13 inches from head to tail. There are several subspecies, all of which have different color patterns. In general these lizards are olive or bluish-gray in color with dark blotches along the back, sides, or both. The eyes are dark in color.

HABITS: This species prefers cooler temperatures and is found in the higher elevations. They are active during the day, searching for the insects, millipedes, and snails that they eat. They will quickly move to shelter under logs, rocks, or forest debris when threatened.

REPRODUCTION: Females give live birth to approximately 10 to 12 young.

RANGE: Includes California and Nevada.

COMMON NAME: **Southern Alligator Lizard**

SCIENTIFIC NAME: *Elgaria multicarinata*

IDENTIFICATION: These lizards grow to a length of 10 to 16 inches from head to tail when adults. Like other Alligator Lizards, they have a distinct fold of flexible skin along their sides that enables them to breathe, since their skin is otherwise tough and hide-like. They are reddish-brown, gray, or yellowish in color with dark blotches or crossbands, depending on the subspecies. The eyes are yellow.

HABITS: This species can climb bushes and trees in search of its prey, which consists of any small animal that it can catch and swallow. Its tail is prehensile— that is, it is able to grasp objects, and is used in climbing. When captured, it defends itself by biting and by eliminating its wastes on the predator. This species finds protective cover in woodlands, grasslands, and especially in groves of oak trees and their debris.

REPRODUCTION: This species of Alligator Lizard lays a number of eggs 2 to 3 times a year when the weather is warm. The average number of eggs each time is 10 to 15, but certain individual females may lay as many as 40 at one time.

RANGE: Includes California.

RELATED SPECIES:
>Texas Alligator Lizard *(Gerrhonotus liocephalus)*
>Features: Larger—grows to a length of 20 inches. Has stripes and

crossbands, especially in the young. Found in Big Bend region in Texas. Moves slowly and purposefully.

<u>Panamint Alligator Lizard</u> *(Elgaria panamintina)*
Features: RARE. Found only in a small, localized area of south-central California.

This Texas Alligator Lizard shows the elongated body and tail and short legs typical of all Alligator Lizards. *(Photograph by Jeffrey Howland)*

LIMBLESS, BURROWING LIZARDS

Family Anniellidae

As mentioned previously, not all lizards have limbs. The misconception has caused some to be mistaken for snakes. However, even though the limbs are not able to be seen externally, if you were to x-ray a specimen of this kind, you would find indications of bony structures that were at one time the limbs of their ancestors.

In the Southwest, only one family of limbless lizards is present, the Anniellids, or the California Legless Lizards. There are several other families of these kinds of lizards native to other parts of the world.

In this family, the lizards are noted for their long, slender bodies that are without external legs, but still contain the pelvic bones within their bodies. Where other related lizards have visible external ear openings, these do not. This is possibly an adaptation to the fact that these lizards burrow in the sand. If they had ear openings, they would likely be full of sand all the time.

If you consider that a burrowing lizard lives completely buried in the sand, you can see that being without legs is a great adaptation for them—they glide along much easier without them. Some of the other burrowing lizards have eyes with specialized lids that allow them to see when the eyelids are closed, while others have no external eyes at all. The California Legless Lizards have eyes as well as moveable eyelids that can be opened and shut as needed without any other adaptations.

COMMON NAME: California Legless Lizard

SCIENTIFIC NAME: *Anniella pulchra*

IDENTIFICATION: This species appears as a shiny, smooth-skinned snake at first glance. They are silvery or tan with dark stripes along the back and sides. The belly scales are usually yellow or cream. One subspecies is completely black or dark brown. They can be distinguished from a snake by their moveable eyelids. They have blunt tails and grow to a length of 6 to 9 inches when adult.

HABITS: They are active primarily in the late evenings and at night, when they are in pursuit of small insects and larvae. They spend most of their time burrowing under the sand or soil, as well as under leaf litter, which they seem to prefer. Some populations have been totally destroyed due to the use of pesticides in the areas where they reside.

REPRODUCTION: Males and females commonly mate in May and June. Females give live birth to 2 to 4 young approximately 4 to 5 months later.

POISONOUS LIZARDS

Family Helodermatidae

In all the world, there is only one family of poisonous lizards, commonly called Gila Monsters and Beaded Lizards. The Gila Monsters, in particular, are native to the southwestern United States, a fact that should make us all stop and consider how important our deserts really are.

Gila Monsters are large, plump lizards that are attractively patterned in red, yellow, orange, and black. They typically have a blunt head, rounded snout, and a thick tail. They have short legs with claws on each toe that are surprisingly strong.

Gila Monsters meander around slowly, flicking out their thick, forked tongues that provide them with a highly sensitive sense of smell. Although usually slow, they can quickly move in any direction, facing their attacker with their large, open mouths and hissing loudly.

These lizards have a potent venom that is secreted by glands located in the posterior lower jaw. Unlike venomous snakes, they cannot strike and inject the venom, but must bite with their immensely strong jaws and "chew" to break the skin so venom is absorbed. The venom produces a painful wound, and if enough is absorbed, can cause death due to its effect on the nervous system.

Yes, it sounds pretty bad, but the fact is, Gila Monsters are not only easy to avoid, a bite from one is very unlikely unless you are in close contact.

Those few individuals who have been bitten were likely trying to pick the lizard up or handle it in some fashion. I don't know about you, but if I came across a big, fat lizard that was hissing with its mouth open, I would think twice about handling that lizard in any way!

If someone is bitten by a Gila Monster, the primary effort should be to remove the lizard as quickly as possible, since the main damage is caused in the chewing of their powerful jaws, which is extremely painful in itself. The best way to remove them is to immerse them completely under water which will cause them to release their grip in order to breathe. As sufficient water is not always readily available in the desert alternate solutions should be considered: wrapping a towel or shirt around the animal's head may cause the Gila Monster to become frightened and release its grip; grasping the animal from behind and pushing it toward the direction of the bite might force the jaws open just enough for the grip to be loosened. Attempting to pry the jaws apart is usually unsuccessful and wastes time. Grabbing the tail of the lizard and pulling strongly sometimes works, but causes severe tissue damage and extreme pain. The best method to deal with a bite is to prevent it in the first place; leave Gila Monsters strictly alone!

Another reason to leave Gila Monsters alone is because they are under governmental protection due to their unique nature as well as their rapidly decreasing numbers. Construction of roads and real estate in areas that once were open deserts has narrowed their habitats greatly. It is therefore quite possible that these animals may one day become extinct.

Gila Monsters are actually quite noticeable when encountered—they are large, plump, and colorful.   *(Photograph by Tom Wright)*

If one is injured by a Gila Monster, they may experience the following:

1. Extreme pain at the site, especially if the lizard has been pulled off. There may be severe bleeding as well.

2. Faintness, sweating, nausea and vomiting, shortness of breath and pallor may occur from the pain itself or from the action of the venom.

3. The venom itself may cause numbness and tingling at and around the site, and the victim may see "blinding lights."

First aid entails:

1. Removing the lizard from the person's body. (See page 77.)

2. Immediate transport to the hospital. Stay calm.

3. Wash the wound with water, and apply pressure to control bleeding. Do not use a tourniquet.

NEVER TAKE ALCOHOL OR DRUGS TO CONTROL PAIN.

At the hospital:

1. Antibiotics and a tetanus injection may be given.

2. Spasms of the artery may be treated with anti-spasmodic medications.

3. An antivenom is under scientific study at present and can be used in extremely severe cases.

COMMON NAME: Gila Monster

SCIENTIFIC NAME: *Heloderma suspectum*

IDENTIFICATION: Their bead-like scales are arranged with a background color of orange, pink, yellow, or reddish hues that are vibrantly patterned with black crossbands and blotches. The face is broad, especially near the posterior jaw, or cheek area, and is glossy black in color. They grow to an adult length of 18 to 25 inches.

HABITS: Gila Monsters are desert creatures and are most active at night and early evening in the summer months. During the day they find shelter from the heat under rocky outcroppings. On warm spring days, they may be seen basking on rocks and, possibly, asphalt roads. In the winter, they hibernate, using the fat they have stored in their tails to nourish themselves. They can go a long time without food, which consists of baby rodents, birds and eggs.

The color pattern of this Gila Monster is the most commonly seen. The Banded specimens are relatively rare. *(Photograph by Tom Wright)*

If moisture is scarce, Gila Monsters are able to use their sharp, strong claws to dig holes in which they lie to stay cool during the extreme desert heat.

REPRODUCTION: Females lay 3 to 5 large eggs in the fall, which hatch approximately 120 days later. Neonates are only 4 to 6 inches long.

RANGE: Arid and brushland areas of Arizona, New Mexico. The Banded forms are also native to some areas of southwest Utah, Southern Nevada, and California.

RELATED SPECIES:

> Mexican Beaded Lizard *(Heloderma horridum)*
> Range: Mexico **(not in our range)**.
> Features: Larger in size than Gila Monsters, but in other respects very
> similar. Coloration is primarily yellow or light orange with black.
> This is the only other poisonous lizard known.

WHIPTAIL LIZARDS

Family Teiidae

Whiptail Lizards are commonly seen and plentiful in the Southwest. They are slender lizards that have long, whip-like tails and a variety of color patterns within the many different subspecies known. Their limbs are strong and well-developed, particularly the back legs. These lizards make rapid, jerky movements, and are quick to take shelter if something threatens them. Depending on the species, adults may be anywhere from 4 to 48 inches in length.

Their smooth skin is made up of small round scales on the upper body and rectangular scales along the bottom. They have good eyesight and a forked tongue that is essentially the organ of smell that locates prey. They eat insects, invertebrates, small mammals, birds, and eggs, depending on the size of the individual lizard.

One of the most unique aspects of these lizards is the way many of them reproduce. In most species, males and females mate to produce fertile eggs. If males are not present, eggs might be laid, but they will be empty of offspring. However, there are a number of species that are considered **unisexual**, which means that all individuals are females and can lay eggs, without mating, that ARE fertile. All the neonates that hatch are females. Male offspring can only be produced when males and females of these species mate, which, in some cases, is a rare occurrence.

COMMON NAME: **Western Whiptail Lizard**

SCIENTIFIC NAME: *Cnemidophorus tigris*

IDENTIFICATION: This is only one species of Whiptail Lizard with the typical slender body structure and long, whip-like tail. Color and patterns vary among the different subspecies as well as among the other related species, which usually have lighter background colors of gray, green, tan, blue, or yellow and darker brown or black spots, stripes, or bars.

HABITS: May be found in a variety of areas including desert grasslands, rocky areas, areas with sparse or abundant vegetation, trash piles, vacant fields, and backyards. They are fast runners and will stalk any moving object in their nearly constant search for food. Many burrow as well in order to find food or shelter.

REPRODUCTION: This particular species produces offspring as a result of the mating of a male and a female and, like all Whiptail Lizards, lays eggs. Many of the related species later described are unisexual, with most or all of the population being female and reproducing without mating.

RANGE: The Western Whiptail Lizard is the widest ranging species; its range includes Colorado, Utah, Nevada, Arizona, New Mexico, California, and Texas.

RELATED SPECIES: The following are several species of Whiptail Lizards that are found in the southwestern states along with those already mentioned. Each species is characterized by different color patterns and range of occurrence. We have presented these different species in this fashion to avoid redundant information.

Canyon Spotted Whiptail *(Cnemdiphorus burti)*
Adult length is 11 to 17 inches, color primarily blue/gray.
Male-female reproduction.
Range: Arizona and New Mexico.

Gray Checkered Whiptail *(Cnemdiphorus dixoni)*
Adult length is 8 to 12 inches, color is dark with a light net-like striped pattern.
Unisexual reproduction.
Range: Small, localized areas in Texas and New Mexico.

Chihuahuan Spotted Whiptail *(Cnemdiphorus exsanguis)*
Adult length is 9 to 12 inches, color primarily brown with light stripes and a bluish-gray or green tail.
Unisexual reproduction.
Range: Arizona, New Mexico, and western Texas.

Gila Spotted Whiptail *(Cnemdiphorus flagellicaudus)*
Adult length is 8 to 12 inches, color primarily greenish or yellow with dark striping, occasional light dots.
Unisexual reproduction.
Range: Arizona and New Mexico.

Texas Spotted Whiptail *(Cnemdiphorus gularis)*
Adult length is 6 to 11 inches, pattern includes stripes down back with spots and a dark chest.
Male-female reproduction. Two clutches laid per year.
Range: Texas and New Mexico.

Orange Throat Whiptail *(Cnemdiphorus hyperythrus)*
Adult length is 6 to 8 inches, color primarily striped with an orange throat.
Male-female reproduction. Two clutches laid per year.
Range: Southern and Baja California.

Little Striped Whiptail *(Cnemdiphorus inornatus)*
Adult length is 6 to 9 inches, with a pattern of slim, light stripes intermixed
    with lengthwise dark bands. Tail brown and blue.
Male-female reproduction.
Range: New Mexico, Arizona and southern Texas.

New Mexico Whiptail *(Cnemdiphorus neomexicanus)*
Adult length is 8 to 12 inches, with a banded and striped pattern and a
    wavy stripe on back. Throat blue-green.
Unisexual reproduction.
Range: Near human habitations in New Mexico.

Colorado Checkered Whiptail *(Cnemdiphorus tesselatus)*
Adult length is 11 to 15 inches. Light stripes as well as heavy black spots
    or bar-like blotches.
Unisexual reproduction, although some males are found, with occasional
    matings taking place.
Range: Southern Colorado, New Mexico, and western Texas.

Plateau Striped Whiptail *(Cnemdiphorus velox)*
Adult length is 8 to 10 inches, pattern of light stripes and black bands. Tail
    light blue.

All Whiptail Lizards, such as this Checkered Whiptail, are identified by their extremely
long, slender tails.   *(Photograph by Jeffrey Howland)*

Unisexual reproduction.
Range: Colorado, New Mexico, Arizona, Utah.

Desert Grassland Whiptail *(Cnemdiphorus uniparens)*
Adult length is 6 to 9 inches. Dark, reddish-brown bands and light stripes.
    Tail olive-green.
Unisexual reproduction.
Range: Arizona, New Mexico, and western Texas.

As you can see, many of the different species are extremely similar to each other in color and pattern. The species we have discussed are not the only Whiptails in this area, and several subspecies have been identified as well. But the ones mentioned are fully representative.

SKINKS
Family Scincidae

The family of lizards commonly known as the Skinks are the third largest family of lizards, with over 500 species known so far. Even though Skinks are found all over the world (except for the arctic regions), they are all surprisingly similar in appearance.

Skinks have a cylindrical, or somewhat sausage-shaped body, with short legs. They are usually shiny in appearance, having tiny, smooth, overlapping scales all over their bodies. All Skinks have a large tongue that is quite wide and notched and is used to find prey in the same fashion as the other lizards and snakes.

Many species of Skinks have developed specializations of their bodies, especially those that burrow. The burrowing skinks may or may not have legs. Some species have a clear area on their lower eyelids, or "window," that enables them to see underground while their eyelids are closed to protect the eyes.

To protect themselves, Skinks are quick-moving and are able to hide efficiently using their coloration to help them blend in or camouflage themselves against the rocks and vegetation of their environments. Some Skinks have brightly colored tails that can fall off, allowing the lizard to escape an enemy. The color is used to deflect the enemy's interest away from the body. Some Skinks have tails that do not come off readily, and many of these will squirm and bite fiercely in order to escape a predator.

COMMON NAME: **Western Skink**

SCIENTIFIC NAME: *Eumeces skiltonianus*

IDENTIFICATION: Adult size is 6 to 9 inches including tail. Color consists of brown or black bands intermixed with light stripes. Juveniles have bright blue tails.

HABITS: These Skinks are active during the day, foraging for insects, spiders, and larvae. They hide under leaf litter, rocks, or fallen logs in the forest or grassland areas within their range.

REPRODUCTION: Females lay eggs, under rocks or logs, and the females tend to them until they hatch. While breeding, males have an orange coloration on head and tail.

RANGE: Includes Arizona, California, and Nevada.

This Gilbert's Skink demonstrates the long, rounded body and short legs characteristic of all Lizards in the Skink Family.   *(Photograph by Jeffrey Howland)*

COMMON NAME: **Gilbert's Skink**

SCIENTIFIC NAME: *Eumeces gilberti*

IDENTIFICATION: Adult length is 7 to 13 inches. Color is brownish-yellow with light stripes that fade with age. Adults are plain brown or speckled. Tail color is orange or red in adults and pink or blue in juveniles.

HABITS: These Skinks are active during the day, sunning themselves on warm rocks or foraging for insects and spiders. They retreat under rocks and logs in the grassland and woodland areas within their range. They are frequently found near small streams.

REPRODUCTION: During breeding, adults' heads turn reddish or orange in color. Females lay 5 to 8 eggs in logs or burrows.

RANGE: Includes California; one subspecies is native to central Arizona.

OTHER SKINKS IN OUR RANGE:

Four-Lined Skink *(Eumeces tetragrammus)*
Range: Texas, New Mexico, Arizona.
Features: Sides with striped pattern, juveniles have blue tail and breeding males have red head. Inhabits arid scrub areas, rocky canyons, and forest areas.

Great Plains Skink *(Eumeces obsoletus)*
Range: Includes Texas, New Mexico, and Arizona.
Features: Largest is up to 14 inches in length. Color is grey or brown with yellow sides. Juveniles are black. Able to eat small lizards, and bites fiercely when caught.

Many-Lined Skink *(Eumeces multivirgatus)*
Range: Includes Utah and Arizona. Separate populations in Texas.
Features: Body long, may be colored with multiple stripes of light and dark. Inhabits desert areas as well as wooded areas in higher elevations.

IGUANIDS

Family Iguanidae

This family of lizards is the largest family, having well over 600 species in different areas of the world. Iguanids are extremely variable in their features and habits, but in general are of moderate size with well-developed limbs and long tails.

Most Iguanids have claws on their toes that enable them to climb trees or to scale rocks. Most of the Iguanids are able to withstand high amounts of heat and are thus more commonly found in desert areas. However, a few species are to be found in cool, mountain climates as well.

Iguanids are well known for their unique ways of communicating with each other. They are extremely protective of their territories and can often be seen defending it against another of their kind with rituals involving head-bobbing and push-ups. Many species will expand their bodies, hold up their tails, or show off brightly colored parts of their bodies to another lizard as a form of defense against a "take-over."

During mating season, the "true colors" of Iguanids are apparent. Not only do many become almost garish in their bright colors, but it is at this time they are most apt to be aggressive in defending their territories. The females of most species lay eggs, and only a few species give live birth.

COMMON NAME: **Collared Lizard**

SCIENTIFIC NAME: *Crotaphytus collaris*

IDENTIFICATION: Yellowish or green in color with blue areas as well as spots and bands. Has an obvious black and white collar on neck. Males have turquoise or orange throats. Juveniles have vibrant crossbands that eventually fade to adult colors.

HABITS: Collared Lizards are active during the day hunting for insects and other lizards which they eat. They grow to a length of 10 to 14 inches. To defend themselves, they will run with the head, body, and tail elevated, and if captured, will bite fiercely. They are seen basking on large rocks, especially in forested, hilly areas and in arid areas where they are able to find rocks with crevices in order to hide and get out of the intense heat.

REPRODUCTION: Females carrying eggs have red or orange spots and bars on the sides of the body. Babies that hatch are approximately 3 to 4 inches long.

RANGE: Arizona, New Mexico, Colorado, Texas, and Utah (depending on the subspecies)

RELATED SPECIES:

Black Collared Lizard *(Crotaphytus insularis)*
Range: Includes California, Nevada, Utah, and Arizona.
Features: Tan or olive with yellow bands on body. Males have black and bluish throats. Found in areas with large boulders and in canyons.

Reticulate Collared Lizard *(Crotaphytus reticulatus)*
Range: Brushland areas of southern Texas.
Features: Reddish-brown with large spots and narrow stripes. Collar is smaller and black. They have a fierce bite and eat most animal matter.

These Collared Lizards are typical of most Iguanids, with their well-developed limbs, colorful pattern, and feisty disposition. *(Photograph by Jeffrey Howland)*

Collared Lizards are named for the presence of black markings on the neck that resemble a collar. *(Photograph by Jeffrey Howland)*

COMMON NAME: Zebratail Lizard

SCIENTIFIC NAME: *Callisaurus draconoides*

IDENTIFICATION: Generally gray in color with spots on body and crossbands on tail. Tail is flattened, with black bars on the underside. Males have blue blotches on the under-side of their bodies. Adult length is 6 to 9 inches.

HABITS: Active during the day, foraging for prey, which consists of anything they are able to catch—insects, spiders, lizards, etc. Some may eat plant matter as well. They are fast runners and are extremely difficult to catch. When startled, they curl their tails to expose the stripes, and may wag them as well. They are ground dwellers and are found in areas with little vegetation and few rocks.

REPRODUCTION: Female lays 3 to 7 eggs in June through August.

RANGE: Nevada, Utah, California, and Arizona.

This Zebratail Lizard is showing an interesting posture—standing high off the tremendously hot ground of the desert.   *(Photograph by Jeffrey Howland)*

This Greater Earless Lizard is very alert and watchful for potential prey, and ready to flee from any predator.   *(Photograph by Jeffrey Howland)*

COMMON NAME: **Greater Earless Lizard**

SCIENTIFIC NAME: *Cophosaurus texanus*

IDENTIFICATION: Adult length is 3 to 7 inches. Gray or brown in color with light flecks. Tail flattened with black bands on the underside. Males have a blue blotch on both sides with black markings as well. No external ears present.

HABITS: Very active during the day. They move rapidly from one area to another searching for insects and defending their territory from other lizards. The tail curves over the back when they run, showing the black bands. They can withstand extreme heat and may even be seen lifting alternating legs to avoid being burned. They are found in rocky cliff areas and dry riverbeds.

REPRODUCTION: Females carrying eggs have an orange throat and slightly pink coloration on sides of body. Females lay 3 to 5 eggs every month from March to August.

RANGE: New Mexico, Texas, and Arizona.

RELATED SPECIES:
Lesser Earless Lizard *(Holbrookia maculata)*
Features: Spotted and striped. Grows to up to 7 inches in length.

Like its relatives, this Lesser Earless Lizard is easily found on rocks, but may burrow in soft sand as well. *(Photograph by Jeffrey Howland)*

COMMON NAME: **Banded Rock Lizard**

SCIENTIFIC NAME: *Petrosaurus (or Streptosaurus) mearnsi*

IDENTIFICATION: Adult length is 8 to 11 inches. Body somewhat flat with a black collar and heavily banded and rough tail. Color generally gray or olive with crossbands and blue or white spots.

HABITS: Active in the morning, scaling large rocks in search of small insects. Will also eat plant matter. Their rock climbing skills are exceptional. They can climb straight upward as well as upside down. The usual posture is to walk with body close to the rock surface with the legs extended in a waddling motion.

REPRODUCTION: Females carrying eggs will have an orange coloration on the throat and over the eyes. Two to 6 eggs are laid in summer.

RANGE: Found among boulders in canyon areas of California and Baja California

RELATED SPECIES:
    Side-Blotched Lizard *(Uta stansburiana)*
    Range: Throughout the southwest.
    Features: Has variable pattern of blotches, stripes, speckles, or spots. Single, dark spot on each side near upper limbs identifies this lizard. Several subspecies known.

The Side-Blotched Lizard is another very commonly encountered lizard. The scale pattern is highly variable.   *(Photograph by Jeffrey Howland)*

COMMON NAME: **Desert Iguana**

SCIENTIFIC NAME: *Dipsosaurus or dorsalis*

IDENTIFICATION: Grows to an adult length of 12 to 16 inches. They have a large, rounded body with a long tail and a row of slightly taller scales on the back forming a crest. They are generally brown or reddish-brown in color with white or gray spots or speckles.

HABITS: They are active during the day and alert and wary to the presence of danger. They are true desert species that can withstand temperatures up to 115 degrees. If rocks become too hot, they will climb onto bushes or low-lying trees to stay cool. They are omnivorous—consuming vegetable matter as well as insects. They are seen in desert brushlands and rocky areas rushing into bushes or behind rocks when in danger.

REPRODUCTION: During breeding season, adults have a hint of pink color on the sides of their bodies. They mate in spring, and females lay eggs at the end of the summer.

RANGE: Nevada, Arizona, and southern California.

Desert Iguanas emerge from burrows in the morning to bask prior to foraging for food.
(Photograph by Jeffrey Howland)

This Desert Iguana demonstrates a long, whiplike tail that is very strong and is often used in defense. *(Photograph by Jeffrey Howland)*

Leopard Lizards are named for their attractive pattern of blotches. They are extremely active Lizards. *(Photograph by Jeffrey Howland)*

COMMON NAME: **Leopard Lizard**

SCIENTIFIC NAME: *Gambelia wislizenii*

IDENTIFICATION: Adult length is 9 to 15 inches. These are slender and large with a generally gray or brown color and dark spots all over the body and on the rounded tail. May have white bars as well. Some subspecies may have white surrounding each dark spot.

HABITS: They are swift and agile, rapidly moving from one bush to another in search of insects. They also consume smaller lizards, for which they will lie in wait in dark areas and capture by surprise. They are found in sandy, dry desert areas with occasional brush vegetation.

REPRODUCTION: Females carrying eggs have orange spots or bars on the sides of their bodies. Eggs are laid in late spring or early summer.

RANGE: Nevada, Utah, Colorado, Arizona, New Mexico, and Texas

RELATED SPECIES:
> Blunt-Nosed Leopard Lizard *(Gambelia silus)*
> Range: Central California
> Features: Color pattern with light crossbars and dark spots. Blunt nose. When in danger, will initially stop in their tracks, then run for cover if approached closely.

COMMON NAME: **Fringe-Toed Lizard**

SCIENTIFIC NAME: *Uma notata*

IDENTIFICATION: Body is flattened. Color is gray with rows of white spots marked with black. Edges of toes have a fringe of pointed scales much like combs. They have scaly flaps over their ears, and their bottom and top eyelids overlap when closed. They have orange markings on their sides, and a black spot.

HABITS: These lizards are active during the day and are efficient burrowers. The fringed toes act to prevent them from sinking in the soft sand. But these lizards are also equipped to burrow and move quickly through the sand if needed. Their nostrils have valves, the ear openings have flaps, and the eyes have specially-closing lids to prevent sand from entering.

Fringe-Toed Lizards are identified by the presence of elongated toes that are edged with comb-like scales. *(Photograph by Jeffrey Howland)*

REPRODUCTION: Females lay 1 to 5 eggs every 4 to 6 weeks throughout the summer.

RANGE: Southern California and southwest Arizona.

RELATED SPECIES:

> Coachella Fringe-Toed Lizard *(Uma inornata)*
> Range: Small area of California
> Features: No black spot on sides.
>
> Mohave Fringe-Toed Lizard *(Uma scoparina)*
> Range: California.
> Features: Crescent shaped spots.

COMMON NAME: **Chuckwalla**

SCIENTIFIC NAME: *Sauromalus obesus*

IDENTIFICATION: Large; adult length is up to 16 inches. Has a large body with a rounded abdomen and loose folds of skin around the neck. The tail is thick and blunt. The front part of the male's body is black, with the posterior colored gray, yellow, or occasionally red. Juveniles have gray and yellow crossbands.

HABITS: One of the "hottest" lizards, its preferred temperature is 95 to 100 degrees. Will bask in the sun until hot, then search for food, which consists entirely of vegetable matter. Chuckwallas hide in rock crevices when frightened, turning themselves sideways and wedging themselves in tightly by inflating their bodies. They are typically found in open areas and around large boulders.

REPRODUCTION: Females lay eggs, some only every other year.

Chuckwallas wedge themselves in crevices and inflate their bodies when threatened.
(Photograph by Erik Stoops)

Tree Lizards are one of the most commonly seen lizards in the Southwest. (See p. 92)
(Photograph by Jeffrey Howland)

COMMON NAME: **Tree Lizard**

SCIENTIFIC NAME: *Urosaurus ornatus*

IDENTIFICATION: Small lizard that has a long tail and a skin fold across the throat, which helps to identify it. Color is brown or gray with dark brown or black crossbands and blotches. Males have patches of blue or orange on their undersides and throats.

HABITS: They are common and are frequently encountered on trees, rocks, walls of buildings, and fences in arid climates. They are shy and will make every attempt to keep much distance between themselves and their enemies. Diet consists of centipedes, spiders, and insects.

REPRODUCTION: Females lay several clutches of 3 to 12 eggs in the months of April through September.

RANGE: Common throughout the southwest except California.

RELATED/SIMILAR SPECIES:

Brush Lizard *(Urosaurus graciosus)*
Range: Nevada, Arizona, and California.
Features: Tail is exceptionally long. Found in desert scrub-brush areas, often rests head down on branches.

Small-Scaled Lizard *(Urosaurus microscutatus)*
Range: Southern and Baja California.
Features: Male has a yellow throat with blue marks on the belly. Found primarily on or around rocky outcroppings.

COMMON NAME: **Short Horned Lizard**

SCIENTIFIC NAME: *Phrynosoma douglassii*

IDENTIFICATION: Has a flat body with a crown or dull spines on the head. The trunk is fringed with pointed scales. May be gray, yellow, or brown with dark spots on back.

HABITS: The numerous subspecies of this lizard make it the most widespread Horned Lizard and the most well-known. It is most active during the day in warm areas. But in areas where it is hot, it is most active in the morning. It eats insects, primarily ants, but can also eat small snakes. May live in altitudes > 5000 feet.

REPRODUCTION: Females give live birth to up to 30 babies.

RELATED SPECIES:

<u>Regal Horned Lizard</u> *(Phrynosoma solare)*
Range: Southern Arizona.
Features: Spines on head large. When caught, becomes rigid and flat and will flop onto its back. In defense, squirts blood from it's eyes. Lays eggs.

<u>Desert Horned Lizard</u> *(Phrynosoma platyrhinos)*
Range: Includes Arizona and California.
Features: Spines on head short. Defends itself by using camouflage. But if caught, will hiss loudly and attempt to bite. Lays eggs, as do those below.

<u>Coast Horned Lizard</u> *(Phrynosoma coronatum)*
Range: Western and Baja California.
Features: Spines on head long. Has spot on neck. Inflates with air and hisses when frightened and may even squirt blood out of the eyes in defense.

This Short Horned Lizard has the typical rounded, flat body of all Horned Lizards, and is the most well known. *(Photograph by Jeffrey Howland)*

This Coast Horned Lizard has a round, flat body, large spines on the head and is well-known.   *(Photograph by Jeffrey Howland)*

Flat-tail Horned Lizards are not commonly encountered. The long, flat tail and slender head spines identify it.   *(Photograph by Jeffrey Howland)*

Flat-tail Horned Lizard (*Phrynosoma mcallii*)
Range: Southern California and Arizona.
Features: Crown scales are long and slender. Tail long and flat. Digs
   burrows using its body.

Round-tail Horned Lizard (*Phrynosoma modestum*)
Range: Arizona, New Mexico, and Texas.
Features: Head crown short, no spiny fringe on body. Has a rounded tail.
   Uses camouflage for defense.

COMMON NAME: **Desert Spiny Lizard**

SCIENTIFIC NAME: *Sceloporus magister*

IDENTIFICATION: This lizard has rough, spiny scales and is yellow or brown
in color with occasional crossbands or spots. Males are usually more brightly
colored with blue patches on body and throat.

HABITS: These lizards are wary and alert during the day, climbing upon rocks
and through ground vegetation while they hunt for insects and other small prey.
Will dart into any available hole or under vegetation to escape their enemies. They
are found in desert areas in low elevations.

REPRODUCTION: Females lay eggs, possibly twice per season.

RELATED SPECIES: There are several species of Spiny Lizards of this genus
in our range, all of which have spiny or rough scales.

Sagebrush Lizard (*Sceloporus graciosus*)
Range: Includes California and New Mexico.
Features: Color greenish or brown with light stripes. Inhabits areas with
   sagebrush such as dry gullies and riverbeds; sandy desert areas.

Clark's Spiny Lizard (*Sceloporus clarkii*)
Range: Arizona and New Mexico.
Features: Slightly greenish-brown in color with black markings on neck
   suggestive of a partial collar. Climbs trees in search of food and
   shelter.

Yarrow's Spiny Lizard (*Sceloporus jarrovii*)
Range: Arizona, south into Mexico.
Features: Has a striking color pattern with light blue or pink scales on

back and a black collar. Inhabits woodland areas of higher elevations. Females give live birth.

<u>Western Fence Lizard</u> *(Sceloporus occidentalis)*
Range: Nevada and California.
Features: Olive, brown, or black with blotches or stripes. Underside colored with blue or orange. Also called the "blue-belly" and is very commonly seen. Inhabits rocky areas, but not in desert climates.

The aforementioned related species are only a few of the Spiny Lizards seen in our range, but are the most commonly encountered. Several other members of the genus, *Sceloporus,* also occur in small, localized areas in our range, but it would be highly redundant to mention them all.

Yarrow's Spiny Lizards have vivid black, blue, or pink color patterns, and reside in mountain habitats.   *(Photograph by Jeffrey Howland)*

— Index —

Bibliography

Collins, Joseph T., 3rd Edition. *Standard Common and Current Scientific Names for North American Amphibians and Reptiles.* University of Kanses.

Stebbins, Robert C., 1985. *A Field Guide to Western Reptiles and Amphibians.* Boston: Houghton-Mifflin Co.

Smith, Hobart M., and Brodie, Edmund D., Jr., 1982. *A Guide to Field Identification: Reptiles of North America.* New York: Golden Press, Western Publishing Co., Inc.

About the Authors

Erik D. Stoops has over 15 years of direct, hands-on experience with the wide variety of insects which inhabit the Southwest. He is the President and Director of the Scottsdale Children's Nature Center for Science and Education. Through the Center Erik annually lectures at 125 schools throughout the country, teaching children about protecting and conserving the animals and plants of the desert. For more information about the Center, write to P.O. Box 6561, Scottsdale, AZ 85261.

Erik's writing credits include ***Snakes and other Reptiles of the Southwest*** (published by Golden West Publishers), as well as additional books about snakes, sharks, dolphins, whales and alligators. Always in the process of researching and writing he currently resides in Arizona.

Annette Wright has more than 10 years of experience with the care of reptiles in captivity. Her main expertise lies in the area of raising young animals, and in providing care to those reptiles that are in need of in-depth care and TLC due to injury or illness.

Both Erik and Annette are advocates of public education as a means to promote the preservation of wildlife. Their goal is to provide the public with information about the real lives of reptiles, in an attempt to dispel fear and misunderstanding of these animals. They sincerely hope that their books will improve understanding and appreciation for reptiles and other living creatures.

RECOMMENDED ITEMS FOR A DAY-LONG WILDLIFE EXPLORATION TRIP

Listed below are items that we recommend for a day trip in the southwestern areas. Consider carrying your gear in a small pack over your shoulders or on your back as weight carried in this manner is less tiring and leaves your hands and arms free for other tasks.

1. Long, strong blunt-nosed stick
2. Whistle (a police whistle is ideal)
3. Good compass
4. Complete first aid kit
5. Salt tablets
6. Strong sun screen
7. Toilet paper
8. Medicines/Prescriptions that you normally use
9. Pocket knife
10. Pencil and paper
11. Lighter and waterproof matches
12. Moleskin (for blisters, etc.)
13. Lip salve
14. Bug spray
15. One day extra food that will not spoil
16. Canteen of water plus back-up supply
17. Extra clothing
18. Plastic bag for litter
19. Raingear
20. Hat, gloves or mittens
21. Sunglasses
22. Maps
23. CAMERA AND FILM!
24. Self Identification

We strongly suggest sturdy, high-topped shoes or boots and FULL LENGTH slacks or pants of a strong material with the cuffs on the outside of footgear.

PLACES TO SEE REPTILES IN THE SOUTHWEST

ARIZONA
Arizona Sonora Desert Museum
Tucson Mountain Park
I-10 Speedway Exit-14 mi. west
Tucson, AZ 85743
(602) 883-2702
Phoenix Zoo
5810 E. Van Buren St.
Phoenix, AZ 85008
(602) 273-7771
Wildlife World Zoo
16501 W. Northern Ave.
Litchfield Park, AZ 85340
(602) 935-9453

CALIFORNIA
Fresno Zoo
894 West Belmont Ave.
Fresno, CA 93728
(209) 266-9543
The Living Desert
47-900 Portola Avenue
Palm Desert, CA 92260
(619) 346-5694
Los Angeles Zoo
5333 Zoo Drive
Los Angeles, CA 90027
(213) 666-4090
Sacramento Zoo
1/4 Mile east of I-5 at Sutterville Rd.
Sacramento, CA 95822
(916) 449-5885
San Diego Zoo
Park Blvd. & Zoo Drive (Balboa Park)
San Diego, CA 92112
(619) 234-3153
Santa Ana Zoo
I-5 and 1st St. (Prentice Park)
Santa Ana, CA 92701
(714) 835-7484

COLORADO
Denver Zoological Gardens (Denver Zoo)
23rd and Steele St.
Denver, CO 80205
(303) 331-4110
Pueblo Zoo
3455 Nuckolls ave.
Pueblo, CO 81005
(719) 561-9664

NEW MEXICO
Living Desert State Park
U. S. Hwy 285
Carlsbad, NM 88220
(505) 887-5516
Rio Grande Zoological Park
903 Tenth Street SW
Albuquerque, NM 87102
(505) 843-7413

TEXAS
Central Texas Zoological Park
Municipal Airport
Near Lake Waco
Waco, TX 76708
(817) 750-5976
Dallas Zoo
621 East Clarendon
Dallas, TX 75203
(214) 946-5154
El Paso Zoo
4001 E. Paisano
El Paso, TX 79905
(915) 521-1850
Ellen Trout Zoo
Ellen Trout Drive - Loop 287
Lufkin, TX
(409) 633-0399
Fort Worth Zoological Park
2727 Zoological Park Drive
Fort Worth, TX 76110
(817) 871-7050
Houston Zoological Garden
1513 Mc Greggor
Houston, TX 77030
(713) 525-3300
San Antonio Zoological Park
3903 North St. Mary's Street
San Antonio, TX 78212
(512) 734-7184

UTAH
Hogle Zoological Garden
2600 E. Sunnyside Avenue
Salt Lake City, UT 84108
(801) 582-1632

RECORD OF SIGHTINGS

Name: _____ Date Seen: _____

Temp.: _____ Time: _____ Location: _____

Observations: _____

Name: _____ Date Seen: _____

Temp.: _____ Time: _____ Location: _____

Observations: _____

Name: _____ Date Seen: _____

Temp.: _____ Time: _____ Location: _____

Observations: _____

Name: _____ Date Seen: _____

Temp.: _____ Time: _____ Location: _____

Observations: _____

Name: _____ Date Seen: _____

Temp.: _____ Time: _____ Location: _____

Observations: _____

Name: _____ Date Seen: _____

Temp.: _____ Time: _____ Location: _____

Observations: _____

More Books by Golden West Publishers

SCORPIONS & VENOMOUS INSECTS of the SOUTHWEST

A user-friendly guide to the wide variety of scorpions and other venomous creatures of the Southwest. Scorpions, spiders, ticks and mites, centipedes, millipedes, bees and more are shown in detailed illustrations and full color photos. *Scorpions & Venomous Insects of the Southwest* by Erik Stoops and Jeffrey Martin.

5 1/2 x 8 1/2 — 112 Pages . . . $9.95

CACTUS COUNTRY

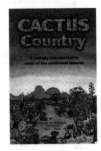

Before you touch, read this fascinating book on cactus of the southwest deserts. The many illustrations and humorous cartoons make this trip through the desert one to remember! *Cactus Country* by Jim and Sue Willoughby.

5 1/2 x 8 1/2—112 pages . . . $6.95

HIKING ARIZONA

50 hiking trails throughout this beautiful state. Desert safety—what to wear, what to take, what to do if lost. Each hike has a detailed map, hiking time, distance, difficulty, elevation, attractions, etc. Perfect for novice or experienced hikers. *Hiking Arizona* by Don R. Kiefer.

5 1/2 x 8 1/2— 160 pages . . . $6.95

ARIZONA OUTDOOR GUIDE

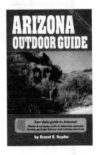

Guide to plants, animals, birds, rocks, minerals, geologic history, natural environments, landforms, resources, national forests and outdoor survival. Maps, photos, drawings, charts, index. *Arizona Outdoor Guide* by Ernest E. Snyder.

5 1/2 x 8 1/2—128 pages. . . $6.95

EXPLORE ARIZONA!

Where to find old coins, bottles, fossil beds, arrowheads, petroglyphs, waterfalls, ice caves, cliff dwellings. Detailed maps to 59 Arizona wonders! *Explore Arizona!* by Rick Harris.

5 1/2 x 8 1/2— 128 pages . . . $6.95

ORDER BLANK

GOLDEN WEST PUBLISHERS

✺ 4113 N. Longview Ave. • Phoenix, AZ 85014

602-265-4392 • **1-800-658-5830** • FAX 602-279-6901

Qty	Title	Price	Amount
	Arizona Crosswords	4.95	
	Arizona Legends & Lore	6.95	
	Arizona Museums	9.95	
	Arizona Outdoor Guide	6.95	
	Cactus Country	6.95	
	Discover Arizona!	6.95	
	Explore Arizona!	6.95	
	Fishing Arizona	7.95	
	Ghost Towns in Arizona	6.95	
	Hiking Arizona	6.95	
	Hiking Arizona II	6.95	
	Hiking Central Arizona	5.95	
	Hiking Northern Arizona	5.95	
	Hiking Southern Arizona	5.95	
	Hunting Small Game in Arizona	7.95	
	Prehistoric Arizona	5.00	
	Quest for the Dutchman's Gold	6.95	
	Scorpions and Venomous Insects of the SW	9.95	
	Snakes and other Reptiles of the SW	9.95	
	Verde River Recreation Guide	6.95	
Shipping & Handling Add ➠	U.S. & Canada	$2.00	
	Other countries	$5.00	

☐ My Check or Money Order Enclosed $

☐ MasterCard   ☐ VISA ($20 credit card minimum)

(Payable in U.S. funds)

Acct. No.   Exp. Date

Signature

Name   Telephone

Address

City/State/Zip

1/96   **Call for FREE catalog**   Snakes

This order blank may be photo-copied.